COMPLEX

PUZZLE

R.C. MCDONALD

Nicholson & Fisher

Maryland

Nicholson & Fisher Publishing
Baltimore, Maryland

Copyright © 2018 by Renee McDonald

Library of Congress Control Number: 2020910793
First Edition: 2017
Second Edition: 2020

Photography by Renee McDonald
Editing by James McDonald Jr.
Cover Art and Design by James McDonald III

Complex Puzzle is purely fiction. Most characters and names have never existed and most events have never occurred. Main characters and businesses are fictious and any resemblance to any person is purely coincidental.

This book is dedicated to my late mother, Annie Marie Fisher Nicholson Camper, my late father Douglass J. Camper Jr. and my late brother, Douglass James Camper III. Each them are in some form depicted in this story.

Chapter 1

Family Matters

A paroxysm consumed my hometown of Baltimore in early 1968 as the city's Negroes reacted to the segregation, unfair police treatment and racial divides of the prior year. It was a time when us Negros were prohibited from enjoying the same swimming pools, skating rinks, bathrooms and other facilities as white residents.

At thirteen, I considered myself a typical teenager and not as a Negro teenager. I loved competing Double Dutch, I loved hanging with my friends and I carried an 'A' average in a challenging school for Negros. To the world I was the happiest kid on Earth and had earned the respect of all who knew me. The racial tensions so many Negro adults complained about did not matter to me; heck life had been that way for as long as I was alive. Though all who knew me enjoyed the large smile I always wore, many never knew the pain hiding behind it. Triggered by the life I lived in the Preston Street row home I shared with my mother, two brothers and three sisters the pain was exasperated every time I stepped into the Hell-hole I called home.

I loved leaving that dark house in the mornings and hated returning to it in the evenings. There were days I'd rather make my way to the Detention Center just blocks away as I felt that the barbaric treatment of the prisoners was an improvement over what I had to deal with.

The actions of the woman who born me seem contradictory to a mother who cared. While she imagined herself as mother of the year her disrespect of those that are force to call her mom demonstrated a strong candidate for Satan of the century. I'll never forget the day my mother, the Queen, gave birth to my baby sister.

It was the coldest day of the year. Very few people were on the streets as I made my way home from school. Those that braved the elements were wrapped in Eskimo clothing, making it difficult to determine the gender of the host carrier. It was so cold that every time I breathe a mouth full of frozen breath filled the air on exhale.

As I approached the three marble steps that led to the old wooden black door of the house I stopped, shivering in fear. Ignoring the impending frost-bite I stood, hesitating as I knew that the moment I touched that worn out door knob I was committing myself to entering the home of Satan. Realizing my life span shortened exponentially with every second in the cold I had no choice but to touch the door knob to Hell. Slowly turning the iron oval shape knob, I tried to enter the house unnoticed. Opening the door, I carefully peeked in to find an empty house. Happy to notice the absence of the Queen my heart rate literally dropped from one-hundred-fifty to a normal sixty-seven. How did I know that, I didn't know, I was just making that up. Anyway, to my dismay a voice was heard from upstairs before I could even lay my books on the old living room side table.

"Kimberly, get up here." A voice yelled.

Not sure of the person attached to the voice I just stood there.

"Kimberly, did you hear me girl" The voice said as I finally realized that it was the voice of our neighbor Mrs. Wilson.

"Yes ma'am." I said quickly dropping the books on the floor then running to The Queen's room.

"Come on, push, push" Mrs. Wilson, a neighbor, yelled repeatedly to my laboring mother as I looked on in fear while my mother struggled to give birth to her seventh child.

I was thirteen at the time and my forty-three-year old mother was giving birth to yet another bastard child. Though it was the seventh child she had given birth to without haven' takin' the vowels of Holy matrimony it didn't bother her that yet again she would be raising another child without the help of its father.

"Kim, Kim get some clean towels", Mrs. Wilson yelled as I stared in amazement as my mother struggled to push.

"Kim did you hear me girl!" Mrs. Wilson yelled even louder.

"Yes Ma'am!" I said as I turned around and practically fell over a nearby chair to hurry to a hall closet where we kept the clean towels.

When I returned from fetching several clean white towels, I suddenly noticed a small fuzzy circular thing appearing from my mother's worn body. The site absorbed my attention leaving me oblivious to everything around me, including the fact that I was carrying 6 towels. As the site drew me closer to the foot of the bed, I unknowingly dropped the towels on the dirty hardwood floor. I couldn't believe what I was seeing. It was the tiny head of a baby, and it was covered in liquid goop and had a head full of black hair.

"Kim, look at you, why in the hell did you drop those towels?" Mrs. Wilson angrily yelled as I just stood there watching.

"Oh, I'm sorry, I'll go get some more." I nervously said before running to retrieve a new stack of towels. It didn't make sense to me as to why I needed to fetch those stupid towels. I guess Mrs. Wilson had watched too many of those old movies because she sure didn't know what to do with the things when I finally got her some.

Moments after returning to the bedroom, the first cries of mother's fifth daughter were heard. It was a tiny little brown skinned baby with a head full of dark black hair. Her skin was covered with all sorts of pinkish goop that had the consistency of a bowl of cooled over tomato soup. Her head was a bit on the flat side as was her nose. Her eyes had me wondering whether her father was of Oriental decent, but the more I thought about it the more I realized that there was no way in hell an Oriental would have been caught dead in that neighborhood. Heck, I didn't want to be caught dead in that neighborhood.

Fixating on the tiny face for several minutes I was still unable to determine which of my mother's last three boyfriends was the father of my new born sister. But later, as I helped Mrs. Wilson clean the baby, I realized she had the nose of Melvin.

Melvin was the neighborhood con-artist and sex addict. On the day my little sister was born it had been months since anybody had seen him. Some say he had been arrested for murder while others thought he had been drafted and sent to Vietnam. Me personally, I believed he had been drafted, after all he was only twenty.

Soon after my new born sister, Mae Jamie Carter, fell asleep next to my exhausted mother Mrs. Wilson grabbed my right arm and dragged me in the hall toward a nearby bedroom. That was the bedroom I shared with my three older sisters, Naomi, Kathy and Beatrice.

My oldest sister Naomi, was and to this day the religious freak. Her love for God had separated her from the rest of the world as most of her time was spent servicing the wills of her savior. She attended church four times a week, spending at least 4 hours there each time. She taught Bible Study, sang on the choir and ran several ministries. Each time she spoke, religious connotations were implied giving me the feeling that my whole life was made up of a basket of sins. Oh, it drove me crazy.

Next was Kathy, the black sheep of the girls, a prostitute. Lamar is Kathy's son by some Jon she slept with when she first started selling her thin dark body for a little bit of pocket change. He looked to be half-white, which didn't surprise me since most of her customers seem to be white. Most of her teenage years were spent skipping school, running with her prostitute girlfriends and hating the world.

Finally, there was the sneaky yet quiet Beatrice. You could say that she talked out of both sides of her mouth. She would tell you one thing but do just the opposite. She felt that if a situation didn't benefit her, she didn't want any part of it. I think she had been around those rich white folks at her preppy rich white school too much. You see, Beatrice was very smart for her fifteen years. So much so that by the age of ten the public-school system had awarded her a full scholarship to a private school in Northern Baltimore city. The school was very exclusive and very few black folks in Baltimore could afford the high tuition. And absolutely no one living on the West side, where we lived, could even afford the uniforms. The City had started this program a few years earlier in an effort to claim desegregation in the schools.

And then there was me, the youngest occupant of this two-bed room. Surrounded by three sisters with three totally different personalities I sort of picked up a little from each of them. Thanks to my three sisters I learned how to live in the city of Baltimore and thanks to my three sisters I learn how not to live in the city of Baltimore. Many days I felt lost and confused but looking to my sisters for guidance was the worst thing I could have done as none of them had any real common sense.

After opening the door to the bedroom, we noticed a sight not meant for young eyes. Laying in one of the twin beds was my sister Kathy with some strange white man laying on top of her. Unaware of our presence Kathy and her stranger continued to have sex before noticing us. Scared he then quickly leaped off Kathy, grabbed a nearby shirt and covered his leaking dick.

"What in the hell are you doin'?" Mrs. Wilson screamed.

"Nothin', nothin'", Kathy said panicking as she quickly reached for a nearby pair of pants and began putting them on.

"Kathy you need to take your il-gotten-ways and that nigger lovin' white man the hell out of your mother's house."

"Oh get out of here you old bat." Kathy replied sarcastically while she continued to get dressed.

"Excuse me you little tramp." Mrs. Wilson said as she rolled her right hand into a tight fist while staring angrily into Kathy's eyes.

"You get on my damn nerves, I'm tired of you mindin' other people's business. So why don't you take your fat ass out of my house and keep it out." Kathy replied as she took a handful of money from the frightened man.

"One-day God will punish you for your sins, you tramp." Mrs. Wilson said as Kathy slammed the door shut after she and her customer left the room.

Mrs. Wilson looked angrily at the door and then began shaking her frail head. After a few minutes of pacing and mumbling to herself she slowly made her way to the chair in which I was now sitting and swinging my long skinny legs.

"Now look young lady, I'm going to tell you this just once. Don't you dare end up like that dam Kathy or that sorry excuse of a mother. You think before you do anything. And you better not go around sleepin' with any and everything that has a dick between its legs. You understand?" She said in a caring yet angry voice.

&

Dear Diary,

The date, December 10, 1967, the time 4:33 p.m. Today was the most awful day. I hated every moment of it. Diary please don't get mad with me for not telling you that The Queen was knocked up. I couldn't believe that she had the nerve to bring another child in this world when she already had six kids that she couldn't raise. Early this morning she gave birth to her seventh child. It was a girl. I can only guess the baby's father. I don't even think The Queen knows. And why should she, to this day most of us have no idea who our fathers are. And Diary, for the life of me I have no idea why she wears that stupid blue scarf every freakin' day.

Douglass, my oldest brother and Kevin my youngest brother are the only ones that know their fathers. Douglass' father, if that's what you want to call him, Freddie shows up every blue moon or so begging for money. Diary you should see the man, begging and pleading and giving these sob stories about losing his job. It always amazed me, just how can you lose a job if you never had one in the first place. Well, at least we haven't heard from that dumb-ass in a while and I hope we never hear from him again.

Kevin's father really isn't all that bad Diary. He does come to see him a few times a week and even takes him shopping allowing me to tag alone. He's really a great father. But what he saw in the Queen at one time, I have no idea.

As far as us girls are concerned, none of us know our fathers. I've asked The Queen several times about him, but

she just tells me to leave her alone. One day I will find out,
but for now I've adopted Kevin's father, Bryant, as mine.
Well Diary, I have to go. The baby's crying, I have to feed
her and make sure she's okay. You know Diary, even though
my mother gave birth to that baby I have a feeling that I'm
the one who will be raising her.

Love

Kim till next time

&

Two months after my bastard sister was born things couldn't have changed more. My sister Kathy was in the women's detention center for selling herself and carrying ½ ounce of cocaine. Douglass had become an active member of a gang called the Black Panthers and I spent most of my time taking care of my little sister. I don't know how I managed to keep an "A" average in school, I guess it was all those late-night homework and study sessions. Man, it's funny how The Queen gave birth to that baby, yet I was the one who got the silver dollar sized bags under my eyes.

To our surprise, Freddie showed up one cold February morning. Drunk and full of spirit he made his way into our humble abode to cause a years' worth of confusion in just a few hours. But it was enough time to con Douglass out of One hundred dollars and make a few passes at me and Naomi. You know, it always amazed me how Douglass had lots of money yet never had a job.

I assumed Freddie, sorry, "Uncle Freddie" knew how Douglass was acquiring his funds but Freddie being the great father that he was just used it to his advantage and didn't give a damn. He was great using any situation to his benefit. Though the Queen was such a hard nose to me she was just as gullible as Douglass because Freddie had no problem using her to satisfy his biological needs. What really irritated me was that Freddie believed that if he couldn't get any on the streets he could always come here and get some. Well, I guess to some point, as long as the Queen lived here he was right. But, despite his other thoughts, us girls were not here for the taking.

Well anyway, that last visit left my mother pregnant once again. She insisted that she wasn't going to have the baby but she had no choice. We were poor so she had no money for an abortion. And anyway, abortions were illegal at the time.

Despite all the normal ghetto drama a couple of good things happened. Because of my grades I was among fifty Negro public school kids chosen to take the Baltimore transition private school scholarship test. That's the same test that got Beatrice into private school. I was so happy when I heard the news, that cold winter day, that I decided to treat me and Kevin to a Cheese steak sub, that was after going home and making The Queen's dinner.

"Well look who we have here, my two favorite kids." Mr. Parkinston said as we entered his store.

"Hi Mr. Parkinston" I said happily.

"Hi Mr. Parkinston." Kevin, my 6-year old brother, said as he walked toward the enormous candy stand.

"So, what brings you kids in today?" Mr. Parkinston asked.

"I just wanted to celebrate." I answered as I sat on a stool in the middle of the long serving bar.

"Oh, a celebration." Mr. Parkinston said smiling.

"Yeah, I was selected to take the Scholarship test."

"You mean the same Scholarship test Beatrice took to get into Friends Mar Academy?" He said with even a bigger smile.

"Yes Sir." I replied nervously.

"I'm so proud of you. You deserve the opportunity to go to such a fine school." He said.

"Thanks Mr. Parkinston." I replied even more nervous.

"And you know you have a good chance of passing the examination, right. You just need to buckle down and study as hard as you can. (Pause) And if you want, I will help you study." Mr. Parkinston continued.

"You know all that stuff?" I asked.

"Well of course I do. I graduated valedictorian from Douglass High School and then later received a Master's from Morgan State College. "

"Wow" I said in amazement.

"I tell you what" Mr. Parkinston said sensing my nervousness.

"To help you celebrate I will cook you one of my famous Cheese steak subs, add a bag of chips and include a bottle of Pop and all for free." He said calming my nerves.

"Do I get some too, I got the lead role in the school play." Kevin asked as he climbed on the stool next to me.

"Well of course my young man." Mr. Parkinston said.

"Yay!!!!!!" Kevin yelled happily.

&

"Hey I'm home" I yelled after returning home from Mr. Parkinson's store.

"Where the hell have you been?" The Queen barked as she sat at the kitchen table stirring a cup of bad smelling coffee.

"We went to Mr. Parkinston's 5 and dime. " I said as I began removing Kevin's coat.

"That's no excuse for you to leave me with a cold ass dinner. I expect my dinner to be hot when I walk into this house and I don't give a damn if you have to watch over this stove for 10 hours until I get home because I want my fuckin' dinner hot." The Queen barked in a high-pitched tone that would win any contest against an adolescent Beagle.

"But it wasn't cold when I left." I said after removing Kevin's coat and walking slowing toward The Queen.

"You're such a stupid child." The Queen said staring me in my eyes as she pushed the plate of food toward me.

"I'm sorry, but what was I supposed to do?" I asked.

"I don't care, next time I expect a hot dinner when I walk in this house. Is that clear you little Bastard?" She so kindly said.

"Yes Ma'am. But Mom I was selected to take the Scholarship test so I went to celebrate." I said hopping for some sympathy.

The silence of the small dark room was deafening. The only sounds resonating throughout was that of the ticks of a nearby clock. There was no movement from The Queen as she sat staring at the old wooden floors. Minutes went by and not a word from anybody. Then suddenly The Queen began shaking her oversized head which was sporting her awful blue scarf, closed her eyes, then looked toward the ceiling. After several minutes, she stood up, walked toward me and stood towering over my tiny body.

"I don't give a damn about that sorry ass test." She said staring me straight in my watery eyes.

Chapter 2

The Woman

That next Sunday The Queen gathered me, Kevin, Beatrice and Mae and forced us to attend the Church in which Naomi spent so much time. It wasn't until years later that I found out why she all of a sudden decided to show her face at the Lord's house when she hadn't step foot in the place since she got knocked-up with Mae. At the time, I thought that maybe she believed that some spirit would recognize her problem and would help her drop her growing bastard child.

As our small group walked the two blocks to the church, I couldn't help but feel self-conscious about the old hammy down outfit I was forced to wear. Not only was the dress an ugly brown and yellow flowered soar eye handed down from my older sisters, but it was an ugly brown and yellow flowered soar eye handed down from a now thirty year old cousin and it was my understanding that she wore that crappy dress when she was thirteen. I figured my aunt must have had a blind person make that ugly dress because the flowers were at least ten inches in diameter, just large enough for a person 2 miles away to make out every raised portion of the many flowers.

To make matters worse the sleeves were way too short for the cold weather and the dress was way too heavy to wear during the summer and way too long for my short skinny body. The bright yellow colored sleeves, which matched the many large flowers, were about two inches long and were thin, puffy, itchy and damn right ugly. The bottom of the dress fell well below my knees and it hugged my slightly mature breast and large butt which made walking a difficult task at best. Its wide bottom made it stylist for 1950 but for 1968 it should have been ripped apart and made into a trash can liner. No, let me retract that. That dress was so ugly that making it into a trash can liner was too good for it, now burning it was the way to go.

The Queen, being the concerned mother that she was, decided that not only should her slave child wear the ugliest dress known to man but she also decided that her slave child needed to stay warm during her walk to church. So, keeping with her stylist ways The Queen forced me to wear a thin green trench coat with large pink buttons on the front to help keep it closed. It would not have been so bad except the coat only hug to my knees thus exposing the ugly dress below. I felt like a crayon box, especially since I was wearing a pair of black patent leather shoes that were two sizes too big and a pair of lime green tights to finish off the outfit.

"Hi Mrs. Carter" A young girl said as she and three other young girls ran from behind us.

"Hi Kimberly" The girl said as the three noted my outfit.

"Hi Jordan" The Queen responded.

"Kimberly, I like your outfit." Jordan said trying to hold

back the laugher.

"Yeah Kim, looks like you took a lot of time picking out that outfit." Another girl commented.

"Leave my outfit alone, I hapin' to like it." I said as I approached the steps to the church.

"Why, you look stupid" Jordan continued.

"You're the stupid one." I responded.

"Boy, aren't we arrogant." Jordan said in a sassy voice.

"Yes, I am arrogant, now leave me alone." I said as I raised my head, turned around and begun walking up the steps.

"Hey Kim, wait for us." The third girl said after the three girls looked at each other in disbelief.

"Yeah." Jordan yelled.

"I can't believe you actually like wearing that ugly outfit." Jordan said approaching me.

"Of course I like wearing this outfit. It was given to me by my famous cousin." I replied lying.

"You don't have a famous cousin." Jordan said.

"Yes I do." I said trying to end the conversation.

"Ok, so who's your cousin." Jordan asked trying to catch me in a lie.

"If I tell you I would have to kill you." I replied.

"Liar, you don't have a famous cousin or you would tell me who it is." Jordan said.

"Try me" I said as I walked close to Jordan and stared her in her eyes without blinking.

"Liar" Jordan replied as she moved so close that the tips of our noses touched.

"Stop playing you two." The Queen said as she walked behind Jordan and me, grabbed the back of our coats and began dragging us up the steps of the church.

Moments later, our group entered the church to find that the service had already begun as the Pastor was now in the middle of a prayer.

"Stop hitting me." I said to Jordan as she poked me in the back.

"I couldn't help it." Jordan said.

"That outfit is so ugly that I just wanted to wash it off your body so you wouldn't be embarrassed when you entered the chapel." She continued.

"I'm going to hit you if you don't shut up." I said in an angry loud voice.

"Kim, Jordan be quiet, everybody's looking at you." Beatrice said.

Jordon and I looked up to notice that the Pastor had stopped his prayer and every member of the church had turned to look in our direction.

"What are yall looking at." The Queen said after noticing an empty pew near the back of the chapel and began walking toward it.

As our group loudly stumbled behind The Queen to the pew, an older woman with a bull nose face approached us. The Queen noticed the well-dressed woman then stopped in her tracks to face her.

"Yes, may I help you?" The Queen sarcastically asked.

"Oh, you're a smart one." The woman said.

"You got that right." The Queen replied.

"Listen Miss. Smart mouth. You need.." The woman started.

"Excuse me..." The Queen interrupted.

"No, you excuse me..." The woman said putting her right hand on her hips.

"Excuse us ladies." Mrs. Wilson said as she approached the group.

"Delores, this is a nasty, nasty woman." The Queen yelled.

"Looks who's talkin." The woman said before taking several steps toward The Queen.

"Ladies, let me introduce you to one another. Mattie this is Delores, Delores this is Mattie." Mrs. Wilson said.

"Oh, I can't believe you actually know this person." The woman said.

"Look whose talkin." The Queen replied.

"Obviously you're an atheist, you non church goin' big ..." The woman said as she began walking toward the front of the chapel.

"Look who's calling the kettle black." The Queen interrupted rolling her eyes.

"Delores, she's the Pastor's wife, so behave." Mrs. Wilson whispered.

Chapter 3

I Don't Get It

My pregnant mother was at her wits end trying to come up with the money to get rid of her unborn bastard. She had been to every relative and friend with no luck. Her brother, Marvin, a Baltimore City Bus Driver, couldn't help her, or should I say wouldn't help her. After Uncle Marvin practically slammed the door in her face, she approached any and everybody she thought had a half a chance of coming up with the four hundred or so dollars for an illegal abortion.

In a way, I felt kind of sorry for her, but I couldn't help think that she deserved what she got. I mean, any woman who had seven illegitimate kids should have learned her lesson before she conceived the eight. Maybe I shouldn't think like that, after all she did keep us all.

With all the troubles The Queen was having I didn't have the nerve to ask her to sign the permission slip to take the scholarship test. But I knew I'd had to find some because it was due back with my homeroom teacher that next day. As I sat outside our run-down home, glazing at all the dilapidated row homes, I thought of ever thing I could to get that woman to sign that permission slip. I even considered signing her name and turning it in without her knowing about it.

"How come I don't have a mother who listens to me and loves me?" I repeatedly said to myself as I contemplated signing the form.

"Hello Kim", A Soft but masculine voice said breaking my concentration.

"Oh, hi Mr. Parkinston" I said coming out of my daze.

"I haven't seen you at the store in a couple of weeks, how are things going?"

"Oh great, great" I said obviously lying.

"Look, when do you want to start studying for the big test, I can arrange my schedule to suit yours." He said in a caring voice.

"Well, I'm not really sure I'm going to take the test,,, I haven't gotten my mother to sign the permission slip." I replied in a low voice.

"What's the hold up, you only have a month and a half to study. Would you like me to go with you to ask your mother?" He said as he sat next to me on the cold concrete steps.

"Yes, if you don't mind". I replied in desperation.

Mr. Parkinston quickly stood and looked lovingly at me as if to tell me that everything would be alright. I then slowly stood, grabbing his left arm with my right hand. After a second or two of thinking I let go of the safety net of his arm then proceeded to open the door.

As we walked into the cold dark living room The Queen quickly runs down the creaky wooden stairs with her size eleven feet flip flapping loudly as they touched every step. I could tell she was angry with me because I could see the smoke coming out of both her devil ears. And the expression on her face, it was so horrid that she could have scared away a hungry lion.

"What the hell is this, haven't I told you never to let strangers in this house." She yelled staring me down.

"Gosh, you're such a stupid child." She continued as she walked toward me and Mr. Parkinston.

"Mom, you know Mr. Parkinston." I said unsure as to why she had no idea who he was.

"We want to ask you something", I said hesitating.

"Oh, we have a question. So you are a we." She said looking at me with those big beady eyes.

"Okay,,, we, " She continued taking a step back and rolling her eyes.

"What is it, I've got things to do." The Queen continued as she reaches her right hand in the right back pocket of her pants.

"Well Mom, I need you to sign the permission slip so I can take the scholarship test." I mumbled.

"Miss. Carter I really think this is a great opportunity for your daughter. I feel as though she will do well on the test with my assistance." Mr. Parkinston said politely.

"Oh give me a break. Kim you don't actually think you have half a chance of passing that shitty ass test, now do you?" She sarcastically said as she lit a cigarette.

"And Mr. Parkinston, what the hell do you want from my daughter. Why are you so willing to help her? Are you some type of child molester or somethin'?"

"Miss. Carter, I have no desires of the kind. I just see how motivated and intelligent Kim is so I would like to do as much as I can to help her live a better life than the one she lives now."

After taking a puff from that awful smelling cigarette she slowly walked toward Mr. Parkinson, stands within two inches of his tall commanding face, looks up some 3 inches to gain eye contact then puts her enormous hands on her ultra wide hips. She then blows a long stream of smoke into his innocent face.

"Get the Hell out of my house." She calmly blurted out.

"Mom!" I yelled.

"And as for you little girl, get your black ass up those stairs and just forget about taking that stupid test!"

"I hate you, I hate you. I wish you weren't my mother and I wish you would die and leave me the hell alone." I screamed running up the steps.

"Do you really think I care how you feel? Now just do what the hell I told you to do." The Queen said walking toward the clock on a nearby wall.

As I ran up the creaking wooden steps I realized just how much I hated that woman. I felt like an idiot for thinking that The Queen would ever do anything for me. How could I have been so stupid? I was a damn fool and a stupid day dreamer.

After storming up the stairs I quickly ran through the door to the room in which I shared with my three oldest sisters. As I entered, I found Naomi reading one of her five Bibles. Deep into her book she paid no attention to me as I slammed the door shut and flopped on the bed next to her. After a few minutes of crying I decided that the only person who really cared was my best friend so I opened the drawer next to my bed, retrieved my diary and began writing.

Dear Diary,

It's February 8, 1968, 4:31 p.m. It's me again. As usual it hasn't been a great day. First thing this morning I realized it was gettin' close to the end of the month and that meant food was getting scarce since Mom only gets paid at the beginning of the month. But that wasn't the worst of it. I had a run in with The Queen, she told me that she wasn't goin' to sign the permission slip for the test and gave me no good reason. Diary she was nasty and she was negative. Diary I really hate that woman, I just hate her. She's always puttin' me down and her mouth, every other word is a curse word. And those stupid cigarettes, I hate them, I hate them. I wish she wasn't my mother,,, I just wish.

As me and my best friend talked about the Queen the door suddenly opens, followed by the Queen storming in. I quickly close my Diary when I realize it was her.

"Here, and I don't want to hear a thing about that stupid ass test again." She said throwing the signed permission slip on my bed before leaving.

Dear Diary,

It's February 8, 1968 4:38 pm. I'm sorry I ended our last conversation so abruptly, but you'll never guess what happened. The Queen, she actually signed the permission slip, can you believe it. I don't know why she changed her mind and I didn't ask either. All I know is that I will be taking the test in a month so I better get studying. I'll talk to you later. Good Bye with love.

Kim

Chapter 4

The Queen

"**K**imberly make me some coffee and it better taste good."
The Queen ordered of me as she, Kevin, Naomi and I ate
breakfast one morning before school.

"But I have to be at school in 30 minutes or I'm going to be
late." I explained.

"Do you really think I care?" She replied staring me down
as I looked frighten at her large shark like eyes.

After gleaming quickly in those horrid eyes, it was apparent
that The Queen was in no mood for the defiance of a thirteen-
year-old girl, to be specific, she was in no mood for me. And
that made it difficult for me to fix a pot of coffee for
somebody who hated my guts and I hated her period. To be
honest I'm not surprised that The Queen didn't care whether
I was late for school or not. I believe if she had it her way, I
would had spent my entire life waiting on her hand and foot.
I wanted so badly to taint her awful smelling coffee with rat
poison or even bleach. But I knew Thunder Thighs would
notice before she died and made sure she knocked me off

before she took her last breath. Man, if only I had the guts to take the chance. But with my luck The Queen would have telepathically sense my deception and then knocked me to kingdom-calm for just considering the thoughts. But despite my cowardliness, I figured there was no harm in dreaming.

"Kim!" The Queen said.

"Yes Ma'am." I answered.

"If that coffee taste like shit you will be making coffee until your stubby little fingers turn blue. So you better make sure you get it right the first time, is that clear?"

"Yes Ma'am", I responded just trying to shut her up.

"Mother" Naomi said.

"Yes Dear"

"Have you decided whether you are going to Dr. King's Poor People's march? Most of the congregation has already signed up." Naomi continued before putting a spoon full of Cornflakes in her mouth.

"Sure Dear, anything for you and Dr. King, Tell Reverend Miller to sign me up and let me know the date of the march so I can let the job know that I will be off that day.", The Queen said as she began walking to the stove where I was reluctantly making her coffee.

After slowly walking tightly behind me she used her 38DD breast to squeeze me between her and that eighteenth-century stove. The more she leaned the harder it was to breathe. She just stood there breathing in enough air so she could fill those oversized lungs. I wasn't sure what to do about that mother/daughter bonding moment so I nervously turned my head to look at her fat man-like face, that fuzzy upper lip and that huge mole on the left side of her enormous mouth. Then it came, eye contact. It was freighting; I just wanted to throw up looking at those golf ball sized red blood-shot eyes. The more I looked in those eyes the more my stomach regurgitated my breakfast and the more I looked in those eyes the more the acids burned the lining of my throat while traveling back down to my stomach. The only thing I could do to stop the cycle was to turn my head back to face the stove and that awful pot of boiling coffee. Oblivious to my struggles she continued to press her breast against my twenty-three-inch-wide body while leaning over my right shoulder to take a whiff of the boiling coffee. With every whiff, she leaned harder and harder as if I wasn't even there.

"Now this is some good smelling coffee." The Queen said. She then retracted her large breasts from my back and headed back to her throne.

"Dr. King hasn't set a date yet. Right now he's organizing just in case he has to march." Naomi said.

"Will the march be in D.C.?" The Queen asked.

"Yes mother" Naomi answered.

"Yeah" The Queen whispered.

"Sign me up. Maybe this will help me get a better job than the crappy waitress one I have now." The Queen then said louder.

"Your job may be crappy but at least Mr. Grayson's nice." Naomi said as I handed The Queen a cup of the extra hot coffee.

"Yeah, he is a good boss. He just pays lousy." The Queen stated while adding a scoop of sugar to the coffee.

"I would like to sign up." I said.

"You can't go; you have a baby to take care of" The Queen said while adding another scoop of sugar to the cup of coffee.

"But she's not my baby." I tried to explain.

"I don't give a crap. You still have to take care of her" She replied before taking a sip of the coffee.

Giving into defeat, as I knew I was fighting a losing battle, I decided it was best to gather my things, get Kevin and head out for school. That woman, if that's what you wanted to call her, had no compassion for me. In my mind, she believed I was her servant and that I was only planted on this earth to suit her every need. At times, I actually believed she was convinced that I had given birth to her last bastard child.

After helping Kevin put on his coat, I thought to myself that one day I would have the courage to tell thunder thighs off and she wouldn't be able to do a thing about it. I couldn't wait to see her puffy eyes get so big that they popped out of her over-sized head. The Queen would one day regret all the horrible things she had me do and said to me.

"Hey family!" Douglass said happily as he entered the house tossing a red ball and heading toward the kitchen.

"Hey little sister" He said slapping me on the back as I stood near the door.

"Hello mother dear" He continued as he walked into the kitchen and before giving The Queen a kiss on the cheeks.

"Where the hell have you been? The Queen asked.

"Oh, here, there, everywhere. No place in particular" He said before reaching into his pocket and handing my mother several hundred-dollar bills.

"Where did you get this?" The Queen asked.

"It doesn't matter mother dear, it's yours for you to use to get you out of your situation." Douglass said putting his right arm around The Queen's left shoulder.

After reluctantly taking the hand full of money she counts it, slowly turns toward Douglass and gives him a puzzling look. She then uses her mighty thighs to stand while maintaining a strong focus on my dear brother. After staring angrily into his beady eyes, The Queen takes his right hand, slaps the money in it then turns around and walks towards Kevin and I.

"What, why, what are you doin'?" Douglass asked confused.

"Look boy, I don't want your death on my shoulder so you take that drug money and put it where the sun don't shine." She yelled.

Shocked by the unselfish act of The Queen I just stood there soaking in the moment. I couldn't believe there was actually a decent bone in that thunder thigh, big breasted, cigarette smoking loud mouth, ugly blue scarf wearing sorry excuse of a mother. I was so shocked at her moment of love, that at one point I was tempted to approach The Queen and give her the biggest, tightest hug ever. But when she looked at me with those big old blood-shot eyes common sense set in so I immediately erase that thought from my mind and headed for the front door.

"Look, I got this for you", Douglass yelled.

"Well you can take it back for me. I will find some other way to handle my problem. Now take that damn money back and I don't want to see it again.", she screamed as she made her way upstairs.

Not sure of what to make of the situation Kevin and I stared at each other in disbelief for several seconds before then heading out the door. As we walked down Pennsylvania Ave. that cold winter day, we noticed a sign on one of the telephone poles announcing that Operation Champ was having a fun day at Kevin's school that next weekend.

"Kim, Kim, can you take me, please." Kevin begged.

"Of course I will. I like it when Operation Champ comes around" I said.

"Me too", Kevin yelled.

"Man, I can't wait to flip on the trampoline, and jump on the balance beam and of course get spotted by Mr. Camper's son." I said while smiling and looking towards the sky.

"Kim, that's all you think about is boys." Kevin responded.

"That's not true, I think about other things too." I said thinking of Mr. Camper's son and smiling.

"Hey Kim, do you think Mr. Camper will let me flip on the mats?" Kevin asked ignoring my last comment.

"Yeah, but this time try not to hit Mr. Camper in the stomach when you do a backhand spring. I felt so sorry for him last time, I mean, I thought the man was actually goin' to die after you knocked him in his stomach."

"Hey, I wasn't that bad", Kevin said.

"I was just joking. Come on, we better hurry up so we won't be late." I said as I began walking faster forcing Kevin to keep up.

"Good morning Kimberly, good morning Kevin" A short stocky man said as he swept trash from in front of Pavilo's Grocery Store.

"Good morning, Mr. Pavilo." I replied.

"Hi Mr. Pavilo!" Kevin yelled.

"On your way to school, I see." Mr. Pavilo stated.

"Yes Sir." I answered.

"You better hurry up, school starts in 15 minutes." Mr. Pavilo said with care.

"Okay." I said as Kevin started running.

"Bye", Kevin yelled running forward.

At the time, Kevin had the energy of an 8-week old Beagle and the tendency to run ahead like one when eager to get somewhere. There were times when I wanted to attach him to a dog's leash just to make sure he didn't run away. I always hoped that he would one day slow down like a fourteen-year old Beagle waiting to meet his maker.

"Come back here." I yelled before he slowed down and waited for me.

After catching up with him, Kevin and I walked quickly passed the businesses along Pennsylvania Ave. where we waved and greeted each storeowner preparing to open their businesses for the day. That is except Mr. Shipiro. Mr. Shipiro was the owner of the Eastern Furniture store located just next to Mr. Parkinston's 5 and dime. Unlike Mr. Parkinson, who was a fine, upstanding black man, Mr. Shipiro was a grouchy old man who acted all of 120 years old. But in reality, he was only 64. Well anyway, Mr. Shipiro never said much to us black folks and when he did, he was quick to use the N word, even to us kids. Because he hated us black folks so much us kids would gang up and tease him to the point where he would get angry and throw buckets of water on us. It was fun and we got a kick out of his frustrations. But for reasons unknown to us black folks, Mr. Shipiro never wanted to close his store and move it to a white area even though most of us didn't want to buy from him.

A couple of minutes after passing the Eastern Furniture store, we arrived at Kevin's school and noticed that the kids had already begun walking in the old brick building.

"Okay, Kevin, you better hurray up" I said stooping down to a level where our eyes met without Kevin having to look up.

As with most days Kevin and I then commenced a good-bye ritual we developed some two years earlier. It was a special hand game we played every morning when I dropped him off at school and whenever we were going to be apart for many hours. First, we would simultaneously perform the sign language for "I love you", then we would open our right hands, bring them together than performed a circular movement. Finally, we kissed each other on the lips and gave each other a long tight hug and then said "Friends forever".

&

After a long day listening to six boring and long-winded teachers I quickly ran home before picking Kevin up from school. As I entered the normally quiet house, I heard Mae crying to the top of her lungs and noticed Douglass sitting lifeless on a living room chair. He seemed to be in a daze and oblivious to the intense crying.

"Douglass" I yelled.

"Why didn't you get Mae?" I continued after slamming my books down on the coffee table next to him.

Unaware of my presence and Mae's crying Douglass continued to sit spaced out and numb to all the commotion. Realizing that Douglass' condition wasn't going to improve anytime in the next century I quickly ran upstairs to tend to my mother's baby. When I entered the Queen's room, this awful smell resonated throughout the room. Hesitant to enter the sickening smelly room I stopped and shook my head in disbelief. I couldn't believe that at thirteen, my life was spent taking care of a bunch of needy and unappreciative lazy black people. I just wanted to turn around and head back out the front door, but with no other place to go I was forced to continue living that horrid life. After taking a deep breath and quickly walking to the crib on the left side of The Queen's bed I carefully picked up the out-of-control screaming baby. And oh, what a juggling act that was. I had to keep her at arm's length as runny brown crap poured steadily out of her soiled diaper. The stench was awful and the half hour cleanup was no walk in the park.

I was expecting that baby to quiet down after her cleanup so I was shocked when she continued to cry out of control. Nothing seem to quiet that baby, even holding her as I walked in circles for five minutes. Looking at the clock, I realized I had only ten minutes to fix the Queen's dinner before leaving to pick up Kevin.

After several more minutes of high-pitched screaming I decided to fix the baby a bottle in hope that it would quiet that deafening noise. And thank God, as soon as she felt the warm bottle of milk in her mouth she began sucking for dear life. Fifteen minutes later and five minutes late for picking up Kevin Mae's stomach was finally full and she had gone quietly to sleep.

Confused as to whether to fix dinner for The Queen or to skip making her dinner and go pickup Kevin. I just stood in the kitchen undecided watching Douglass transition into another world. It was sickening seeing an eighteen-year-old man laying clueless on a tattered old chair in a dark room with the television staring at him. Well it was a no brainer, picking up Kevin outweighed the need for the Queen to have a hot dinner when she arrived home.

When Mae, Kevin and I returned home the Queen was sitting impatiently in the living room on a couch next to the chair where Douglass had now passed out. The Queen stared me down as I walked through the door. Her fixating eyes gave me the he-me-geemies. Her manly right hand tapped quickly on the neighboring side table and her size eleven right foot tapped in sync with her hand while those eyes followed my every move.

After quietly setting Mae on the couch next to the Queen I helped Kevin take off his coat before he quickly ran to the upstairs bathroom. Scared, I slowly made my way in the living room as the loud noise of the second hand of the hanging clock ticked loudly.

"Kimberly" The Queen said in the angriest tone.

"Yes Ma'am" I quietly said ready to throw up in fear.

"I was very upset that my dinner wasn't ready when I got home." The Queen continued.

"I'm sorry, but when I got home Mae was screaming so I had to tend to her and by the time I was finished it was time to pick up Kevin." I explained.

"Dam it, you should have made my dinner while you were dealing with that baby." She yelled, standing up.

"But I couldn't because I had to change her diaper and give her a bath. Then I had to feed her because she wouldn't stop crying." I cried in anticipation of a fast slap across my face.

"No, you just didn't want to make my dinner." She replied angrily as her large frame approached me.

"Let me tell you something little girl." The Queen continued.

"The next time I come home and my dinner's not ready and hot I'm goin' to tear you from limb to limb. I will not have any mercy. I will not hold back. I will just tear you apart. Is that clear?" She said shaking her right index finger in my tiny scared face.

"Yes" I said in a low voice while holding back the tears.

"What, I didn't hear you?" She said in a Drill Sargent's tone.

"Yes!" I said louder.

I quickly walked into the kitchen and began preparing dinner. I was so scared I kept my coat on as I searched the refrigerator for a meal suitable for a Queen of her caliber. After pulling out a package of defrosting chicken wings Kevin runs down stairs, walks through the living room and joins me in the kitchen. Looking at me puzzled, Kevin stops at the table to analyze me from head to toe.

"Why don't you take your coat off?" Kevin asked.

"Because." I said not willing to reveal my real reason.

"Because what?" He continued.

"Just because." I said as tears began flowing uncontrollably down my cheeks.

"Kim", Kevin said approaching me.

"Why are you crying?" He asked as he walked to me then hugged me.

"Kevin, let her finish making my dinner." The Queen demanded.

"But she's crying." Kevin explained.

"That's because she feels guilty for not fixing my dinner?" The Queen said as she leaned against the wall that separated the kitchen from the living room.

Frustrated Kevin walks to The Queen, balls up his tiny right hand and uses it to hit The Queen in her overly stretched stomach. I wanted to run and grab him to save him from the Anaconda grips of thunder thighs. But for some reason I decided to see what the now angry bulldog was going to do to my baby brother.

"Why are you being so mean to my sister." Kevin yelled.

"I beg your pardon little boy." The Queen said looking shocked.

"You always act mean to Kim, now stop." Kevin insisted.

"Look little boy, leave me alone before I get my switch and beat your butt."

"I don't care, just leave my sister alone."

"Kevin" I yelled wiping away the tears.

"Don't yell at her. She might hit you." I warned.

"I don't care." Kevin continued.

"Little boy, upstairs now." The Queen yelled.

"No!!" Kevin angrily replied.

Upset over the sudden outburst of her youngest son, The Queen lays grabs Kevin by his right hand. She then picks his small body off the floor and carries him towards the stairs to the second floor.

"You better not hurt him." I yelled dropping the package of chicken on the kitchen floor.

"You dare yell at me?" The Queen said irate as she looked impatiently at me.

"I hate you. You are the worse mother I've ever seen in my life. Why..." I continued.

"Why what?" She screamed to the top of her lungs.

Afraid of the consequences from further upsetting the Queen I froze, stared and shut up. The room was quiet and that awful loud clock continued to tick. One second, two seconds, ten seconds then thirty seconds went by before a move was made. Finally, right before the clocked ticked thirty-one seconds The Queen put Kevin down and began walking up the creaking stairs.

"Let me know when my dinner is ready." She said in a calm voice focusing on the stairs.

&

Dear Diary,

It's Feb. 10, 1968 7:30 p.m. How are things with you, things are the same with me. School's getting harder and thanks to my mother's baby I have to do my homework in the middle of the night. Sometimes that baby keeps me so busy I don't get much sleep before I have to get up and get me and Kevin ready for school.

Diary, even though I have tons of studying to do and lots of homework I love school. It gives me a break from the slave treatment I get at home. The only good things about home are playing with Kevin and talking to you. Thanks to you and Kevin I can forget the rest of my sorry excuse of a family. They all seem to move to the beat of different drums, driving me crazy as they go about their daily lives. Diary, it's amazing that we even know each other's names because we rarely see each other and when we do see each other we hardly speak. And the conversations we do have seem to resemble a verbal boxing match more than a friendly family conversation.

I'm so sorry Diary for laying all my troubles on you, but The Queen is really getting on my nerves. I'm sick of being her house slave and I'm sick of being her daughter. Today she yelled at me for not having dinner ready when she got home. Well, ,,,you know what, I should have let her sorry butt starve to death. I know with all that fat it would have taken a year or two for her to croak, but at least it would have been a start. Why does she treat me so badly Diary, why? I've never done anything to her. I'm the only one in this house who does anything for her. I cook for her, I clean for her and I take care of her crying baby, what more does she want. Why does she hate me so much?

Kim.

Chapter 5

Okay Then

The day Kevin had anxiously awaited finally arrived; it was the day Operation Champ came to his elementary school. I will never forget that day. It was an abnormally cold day, the temperature hovering just around twenty degrees with a threat of snow. The winds were blowing at about thirty miles an hour., making walking difficult. It was the worse day of the year but that didn't squash Kevin's excitement. Normally Kevin would roll out of bed around 10:00 a.m. on Saturdays but that day his excitement had him up and at the foot of my bed at 7:00 a.m.

"Kim, wake up." I heard him say as I dreamed of me and Michael Jackson kissing.

"Kim" he repeated.

"Kevin, what are you doin?" I said slowly waking up.

"It's almost time to go." Kevin continued.

"But it's only 7:00" I wined after taking a glimpse at a nearby clock.

"I know, so we only have three hours before it starts."

"But I want to sleep for another hour." I replied turning over.

"Okay, I'll just stay here until you get up." He said before sitting at the bottom of my bed staring me down like a wolf sizing his prey.

At the time, Kevin had the patience of a twelve-year old Hound Dog waiting for his maker. So, instead of fighting, I gave into his excitement and slowly made my way out of bed. Though my intent was to get the two of us ready then relax in the living room before leaving we ended up spending more time laughing and playing trying not to wake the rest of the family. But despite our best efforts we failed to do a very good job because moments before going downstairs the Queen Bee came out of her hive and began stinging.

"What is all this noise?" She asked.

"Operation Champ is coming to my school today." Kevin replied

"Yeah, we're leaving at 9:00" I said.

"Who said you could go?" The Queen asked putting her hands on her large hips.

"I just figured there wouldn't be a problem if I took him." I explained.

"What did I tell you about thinking. Every time you come up with these great thoughts you get yourself in trouble. "The Queen said.

"But we want to go." Kevin wined.

"But we want to go." The Queen said in a wining voice teasing Kevin.

"Stop teasing me!" Kevin yelled.

"You know little boy, your mouth is getting a bit large for your small body. If I were you, I would shut up because in a minute I'm going to send you outside to that tree so you can pick yourself a switch." The Queen threatened.

"So we can't go?" I asked.

"Very good." The Queen replied with a smirking smile.

"Why, I wanna go." Kevin cried.

"Kevin, Mom said we can't go. Let's just go downstairs and clean the kitchen or somethin'."

"No Kim, I wanna go!" He screamed.

"Don't worry, we'll have just as much fun here." I said lying.

"No I wanna' go." Kevin screamed getting more agitated and jumping up and down like a two-year old.

"Shut up little boy." The Queen yelled.

"No you shut up!" Kevin screamed louder.

"Hey, what's all the noise, its 7:30 in the morning." Naomi said entering the hall from the bedroom we shared.

"Operation Champ is at Kevin's school today and Mom won't let us go." I replied telling on the Queen.

"That's because you are bad kids and bad kids shouldn't get what they want." The Queen said.

"Mom, you should let them go." Naomi said.

"Hell no. Kim has to take care of Mae and make breakfast and clean this filthy house." She said trying to justify her decision to make my life a living hell.

"But I just cleaned the house yesterday." I explained to Naomi trying to win an ally.

"Yeah, and you didn't do a very good job." The Queen defended herself.

"Mom, don't be so hard on her. She does more around here then all of us put together. Let them go, I'll watch the baby if you need help." Naomi said defending us.

"Ok", I said to myself. "Let's see what big hips has to say about that comment." I continued to myself.

Staring at the Queen's big OLE eyes and waiting for her response to her favorite child's comment I just knew she wouldn't disappoint Ms. God. "I dare you to cross her." I said to myself. "I just dare you." I continued over and over again in my head.

"Alright, only because you asked." The Queen said after a long pause.

"I knew it. The Queen never says no to Ms. Naomi, the Goddess of Preston Street." I said under my breath.

"Yay, thanks Naomi!!" Kevin said giving Naomi a tight hug.

I refused to say anything to either Naomi or the Queen. I was pissed at my sorry excuse for a mother's negative attitude toward me and Kevin. And it became even more obvious that early Saturday morning that the Queen thought less of me than the roaches that take over the kitchen at night. I found it amazing how she listened to every word Naomi said yet acted like I was just some stupid idiot. I was so pissed that I grabbed Kevin's arm and lead him down the stairs to get the hell away from her and her nasty attitude. The Queen could tell that I was upset, and you know what, I don't even think she cared because I swear I heard her laughing at us as when we reached the bottom step. To be honest, if Kevin wasn't there that woman would have been a goner. "Bitch" I said looking upstairs as Kevin runs into the kitchen.

After calming down and waiting almost two hours Kevin and I left for his school. We were one of the first to arrive at the school's gym. Because we arrived ten minutes early, we were forced to wait at the door until Operation Champ was ready to let us in.

To our surprise there was already a line of thirty or so kids waiting to get in. This didn't sit well with Kevin. Dag, the boy complained the entire time we waited for the doors to open.

Finally, when the doors opened the crowd ran into the transformed gym of the ancient elementary school and disbursed to the different stations. On the left side of the gym was a station with a couple of portable basketball nets, a volley ball court and a few jump rope stations. On the right side of the gym, there were several food stations ready to serve hot dogs, sodas, pizza, and all sorts of fattening foods. It was a junk food junkies' heaven. And best of all Operation Champ had set up the center of the gym with two trampolines, a few tumbling mates, a couple of balance beams and a set of parallel bars.

"Mr. Camper!" Kevin yelled happily as he ran toward the event's organizer.

"Hey Kevin, I knew you would be here." Mr. Camper said as the two approached each other.

Mr. Camper and Kevin were like two old best friends who hadn't seen each other in years. The two of them talked for over twenty minutes catching up on the past year. I could tell that Kevin bonded with Mr. Camper as if he were his father. The conversation went from Kevin's grades to cartoons to Kevin's future. That was the one thing about Mr. Camper he had a way with talking to kids and he seemed to care about us all.

As Kevin and Mr. Camper chitchatted my eyes focused on the extra-large trampolines. There were two just waiting for me. I could hear them calling my name "Kim, Kim", they kept calling. Knowing the lonely trampolines missed me, I decided not to keep them waiting any longer. You know I loved Kevin and all but those trampolines were way too inviting and besides, there was nobody in line. But by the time I got to the trampolines there were ten kids lined up. Man, I was mad, I actually had to wait and it was a long wait. It was ignoring how those kids actually acted like they were training for the Olympics. Marcus, one of my classmates since third grade and class irritant, was the worse one of them all. He must have stayed on my trampoline for more than fifteen minutes. And oh did he think he was good, you should have seen that smirk on his big scared face every time he flipped. Man, he was getting on my nerves and I was just waiting for him to flip off that trampoline and fall flat on his face. But as always, my dream failed to come true as he performed a perfect routine.

After thirty minutes and three people it was my turn. Confident, I was eager to show off Mr. Marcus Pope. I couldn't wait to put a smirk on his tired looking face and show him just how sorry he was, compared to me that is. He didn't know it but the previous year I could flip better than he could that day. As a matter of fact, Mr. Camper had asked me to join his gymnastics team because I was so good.

I was looking forward to seeing Mr. Marcus put his tail between his legs in embarrassment. I was ready when I climbed onto the trampoline and begun jumping slowly to get use to the tension of the bed. Next it was time to show off and put the others to shame. To start, I decided to begin with a simple front drop to a back drop then some swivel hips. After that I'll perform a combination of front flips, back tucks, back pikes and a few layout fulls. As I jumped, I realized that the best way of getting the momentum for my routine was to jump as high as I could for a couple of minutes while focusing on every body position. With each bounce I got higher and with each bounce I became more comfortable with my abilities to perform my routine.

When the moment came to start the routine, I stretched my body to a horizontal position at the top of a bounce in preparation of performing a front drop. I was happy, I was confident and I was lookin' good. The built-up momentum was sufficient to complete the front drop and then immediately perform a back drop.

"Ah yes" I said to myself as my completely horizontal body approached the trampoline's bed.

"Ouch!!" I yelled in pain when the front of my body came in contact with the trampoline.

"Kim, what's wrong?" Mr. Camper yelled from across the gym as I stood up, grabbing my chest and walking cautiously to the front right edge of the trampoline.

"Nothing Mr. Camper, I'll be okay" I said in an effort to hide the pain.

"Are you sure Kim?" He asked as Mr. Marcus Pope burst out laughing.

Oh my goodness, in all my long thirteen years of existence that was the worse pain I had ever experienced. My breast hurt like crazy. You know I never thought twice when my bra size went up two sizes that year. But I was determined to show off Mr. Marcus Pope, as he laughed loudly at my sudden pain. So, I started my routine again, ignoring the pain of my bouncing 32c breast.

Ten minutes later I cleanly completed by routine of many tricks and flips. By the time I was done, that laughing smirk from Mr. Pope had turned into a face of envy. Not only was he speechless but he couldn't even look me in the eyes as I climbed off the trampoline. I had shown Mr. Marcus Pope and everybody else just how good I was. I showed them how do to perfect front flips, back flips and yes, side flips. I was so good that when I got off, I confidently walked to Mr. Pope, looked him in the eyes, and said "Huh" as I raised my head royally. I then accented my great performance by walking like a champ pass the waiting crowd and proudly walked to the girls' bathroom where I quickly grabbed my throbbing breast and began crying from the intense pain. After examining them in one of the dirty stalls, I noticed they had turned a bright red and were numb to touch.

"Oh well" I said to myself "I guess this is the last year I can do trampoline." I finished. "Man, puberty sucks." I thought.

The next few hours were spent learning to survive on a four-inch-wide piece of wood, hanging and gossiping with friends and staring at the cute boys working with Operation Champ. Time flew by. When Kevin and I arrived, it was 10:00 a.m. and now, before I knew it, the time had passed to 2:30 p.m., without eating.

"I'm hungry, let's get a slice of pizza." Angela, a good friend, said.

"Yeah, I'm hungry too." I replied.

"Kevin!" I yelled.

"Are you hungry?" I continued.

"No" He yelled after his 100th flip.

"Okay, I'll be over there eating" I said pointing to the roll of tables near the back of the gym.

"Alright" Kevin said out of breath.

Angela and I walked to the concession stand, grabbed a couple slices of pizza, a bottle of soda pop and a bag of chips. We then took our healthy meals and sat next to a couple of kids from the neighborhood. Sitting at the small cafeteria style table were Darlene Montgomery, one of my very best friends and rival ninth grade valedictorian with several other neighborhood kids. Darlene and I had been friends and rivals since kindergarten. We both had "A" averages and we both skipped second grade. Darlene and I both loved Double Dutch and at the time we competed on the same city team.

But that's where the similarities stopped. Darlene was from a very respectable family. She had one older brother who at the time was attending Morgan State College in East Baltimore. Like Darlene he also earned a perfect "A" average through school. At the time, it was my understanding that he was a member of the National Honor Society at Morgan. Unlike my removed mother, Darlene's mother was always involved with her activities. She was always volunteering in their schools and was present and cheering for Darlene at every Double Dutch competition, spelling bee and science fair. Her father had been PTA President since Darlene entered kindergarten. My father on the other hand was nowhere to be found.

"Hey" I said.

"What's new" Darlene asked.

"Nothing" I replied sitting down.

"I like when Operation Champ comes around, there's always lots of free food." Angela said.

"Not to mention, Mr. Camper's son Derrick. He's so cute." I said.

"For real" Darlene responded.

"He's way too old for yall." Angela said.

"Who cares", Darlene said.

"Your mother would never let you go out with a seventeen-year-old." Angela continued speaking to Darlene.

"She doesn't have to know." Darlene said.

"Your parents know everything you do, un-like my mother." I said.

"Yeah Darlene, every time we see you, we see your mother, see.", Angela said pointing to a tall slender woman sitting at the nearby registration table.

"She gets bored at home so she volunteers for everything, it gets on my nerves sometimes."

"Yeah, my mom volunteers for everything too, but I really don't mind." Angela said.

"I wish my mother would come to some of my school stuff. Man, my mother's so out of it I don't even think she knows where I go to school." I said.

"Hey girls", Marcus cheerfully yelled as he and a group of boys approached the table.

"What do you want Marcus?" I asked.

"Hey, have you guys ever seen those barrels in the Frank's garage." Marcus asked.

"Yeah, who hasn't?" I replied.

"Don't you want to know what's in those things." Marcus continued.

"Never thought about it." I replied.

"Me neither." Darlene agreed.

"Figures, you girls are so stupid." Marcus said.

"Who you callin' stupid?" Darlene asked.

"Well we want to know what's in them." Marcus replied.

"So why you tellin' us?" I asked.

"Because tonight we're gonna' break into their garage and take the barrels to the open lot behind the old church."

"So?" I asked waiting for a reason why I should care.

"So?" Marcus said.

"Because we want you guys to help." He continued.

"Heck no." Darlene said as she notices her mother approaching.

"Darlene dear, it's time to leave now." Mrs. Montgomery said.

"Yes Ma'am"

"Hi Mrs. Montgomery", I said.

"Hello Kimberly, how are you today?"

"Fine."

"Great. By the way I would like to invite you over for Darlene's birthday dinner next Sunday. Do you think you can make it?" Mrs. Montgomery said.

"Yes, I would love to come."

"Great, dinner starts at 5:00, I will see you then."

"Okay"

"Bye guys." Darlene said as she and her mother walked away.

"Alright, are you girls in." Marcus asked.

"I'm in" Angela said.

"I don't know." I said hesitating.

"Come on Kim, stop being such a goody two shoes." Marcus said.

"It'll be at night, right?" I asked.

"What difference does it make?" Marcus said.

"Yeah Kim, it's not like we're gonna' get caught." Angela said.

"Okay." I reluctantly said.

I knew what I had just agreed to was wrong. I knew I didn't want to be a part of what was about to happen but, for some reason I just couldn't say no. But just the thought of getting caught scared the hell out of me. I could just see the Queen's face if I got caught and it wouldn't be a pretty sit. But you know what, why not prove The Queen right when she calls me a bad kid. Hey, I figured I may as well live up to her expectations.

During the walk home, I tried my best to think of every lie I could to get out of that house. I thought of telling the Queen that I left something at the school and had to run back and get it, like she would fall for that. I also thought of sneaking out of a window, but the upstairs windows were too high. I could climb out a first-floor window but the Queen spent most of her time in the kitchen feeding her thunder thighs. No matter what, I knew in order to meet the group I had to think of something quick because they were expecting me at the Frank's house in less than fifteen minutes after returning home.

As Kevin and I entered the house my heart began pounding and my hands began sweating, all in anticipation of the Queen's foul mouth. As I closed the door, I found Naomi sitting on the couch, reading a Bible in an abnormally quiet house.

"Hey" I said.

"So how was Operation Champ?" Naomi asked.

"Great, we had a blast" I said waiting for big hips to appear and begin ordering me to clean the windows with a tooth brush or something.

"Kevin, did you get a chance to flip?" She asked.

"Yeah, and I didn't even kick Mr. Camper."

"That's great. Did you learn any new tricks?"

"Yeah, Mr. Camper taught me how to do a back tuck."

"Man, one day you'll be good enough to go to the

Olympics." Naomi continued

"I never saw a Negro do gymnastics in the Olympics." Kevin said.

"Well, you will be the first one, how about that?" Naomi said with confidence.

"So, where is everybody?" I asked looking around.

"Well Douglass is out as usual; Beatrice is upstairs studying and Mother took Mae to Uncle Marvin's house."

"So, when is Mom coming home?" I replied realizing my chance to exit without hell was handed to me on a silver platter.

"I don't know, she just said sometime after 9:00."

"Oh" I said thinking that I could meet with my friends and get back well before the Queen returned home.

"Naomi, since Mom's not here, I'll ask you. Mrs. Montgomery invited me for dinner, is it okay if I go? I'll be back by 7:00"

"That's fine with me."

"Thanks" I said happily.

"I'll see you in three hours." I said with excitement.

"Okay, don't forget to thank the Montgomery family for having you over."

"I won't." I yelled heading out of the front door.

Moments later I joined Marcus and group a couple of doors away from the Frank's garage. Thank goodness the Sun had already gone down so it was hard for anybody to see what was going on. In my mind the darker it was the less chances of somebody recognizing me. Also, in my favor, was that the group was double in size then I thought it would be making it easy to hide. At first count, there seem to be more than fourteen kids, all ready to commit the crime of the century.

"Come on let's go." Marcus said walking toward the Frank's garage.

As instructed the entire group lined up behind our infamous leader and headed toward the Frank's garage. The members of the group looked as if they were a bunch of ducklings following their parents as they crossed a busy street. That was everybody except me. At the last minute, I chickened out and hid behind a tree in a nearby yard. Without notice, I watched the group walk toward the seven barrels located in a garage just two houses down. After Marcus led his little ducklings to the barrels, he instructed the group to divide into seven teams of two and to begin moving the barrels to the vacant lot in which they all just left. The barrels stood about four feet high, about eighteen inches in diameter and were dark in color. Most teams struggled as they loudly rolled the seven barrels down the dark alley.

After twenty minutes of constant bickering amongst the group's members the last team rolled their barrel into the vacant lot. As they attempted to open the first barrel my instincts were telling me to leave, that I had fulfilled my promise and showed up. At that moment, I knew it was time for me to get home and let the thieves enjoy the fruits of their labor, but I was curious as to the content of the barrels. I just wanted to see what was in the first one then I would be on my way. But, before the first barrel was opened several cars quickly turned into the dimly lit alley from a nearby street. After the speeding cars stopped several Police jumped out of each car and pointed their guns at the unsuspecting group.

"Get away from those barrels Niggers." One of the Policemen yelled.

Most of the kids followed the orders of the demanding

police officers, but Marcus and his two goof-ball followers Bunny and David dashed for a nearby chain linked fence, and that's when it happened. Marcus was shot many times as he attempted to climb the six-foot-high fence that separated the alley and from the neighboring yard.

The sounds of the firing guns reminded me of the dramatic images of the Vietnam War. Those images horrified me on t.v just as this horrified me. There was blood everywhere and the scene was one of confusion. Like the Vietnam War news stories, there was a mass of confusion. The rest of the kids began screaming and some even attempted to run.

From a distance, I could see parts of Marcus's brain slowly land in several places on the cold trashy yard. In my mind, it took Marcus' body several hours to lose its grip on the chain linked fence and fall to the ground. The sound of the falling corpse rang loudly through the air causing great pain in my ears.

Instinctively my hands began piercing the bark of the tall thick birch tree. My skinny long fingers began to numb as they slowly dug deeper into the hard bark. After several seconds of digging my fingernails had filled with thick pieces of bark causing all but one finger to bleed. But I kept holding on for dear life while attempting to remain out of the sites of the many police officers.

Thinking that the shooting spree was over I slowly began to ease up on the tree, but then several more shots were fired at Marcus' lifeless body.

"Ahhhhhhhh!" One of the girls yelled as she covered her eyes.

In an instant, his already unrecognizable face had been blown into a hundred more pieces. Apparently, with no remorse, the officer then nonchalantly approached the fence where Bunny and David were attempting to climb.

"You Nigger's better stop or you will end up just like him." The Officer yelled at Bunny and David.

Bunny and David abruptly stopped, then slowly turned toward the trigger-happy Police Offer.

"Get the hell off that fence and put your damn hands up Niggers!" The Officer yelled.

Bunny and David quickly jump off the fence and put their hands in the air in an effort to keep the Police Officer from shooting.

"Get over there with the rest of those Niggers." The Officer ordered of Bunny and David.

The two did as they are told while keeping their hands up and above their heads.

"Please don't shoot." Bunny begged.

"I'll shoot if I want to. Now shut the hell up."

"Yes sir." Bunny cried as his frail body begins to shake.

"Alright, lets take em' in." The trigger-happy officer yelled to his counterparts.

After witnessing the murder of a friend, the group was then quietly forced to walk quickly to two awaiting patty wagons. As the group approached them they were split into two groups, separated by sex, girls in one line and boys in the other.

"Oh my God" I thought to myself.

"Please God, let me get out of this without those crazy police noticing me, please." I continued to myself.

"If the Queen finds out about this, I'm dead." I thought as I began gripping the tree harder.

As the last girl was loaded into the Patty Wagon my grip on

the tree began to loosen. I couldn't wait to get home and see the Queen after seeing all that mess. For the first time in my life I was looking forward to seeing the woman known as my mother. I really couldn't believe I was saying that, but I actually wanted my mommy. As the doors to the first patty wagon began to close, I began to relax. But, to be on the safe side, I figured I wouldn't leave for a few minutes after the last patty wagon left. Finally, the first patty wagon, caring the boys, left and then the police began to close the doors to the second patty wagon caring the girls.

"What are you doing?" A strong voice said as I realized the barrel of a gun was now on the back of my neck.

The tight grip on the tree returned and my bleeding fingernails were now solidly pressed against it. Impatient for an answer to his question the Police officer used his free hand to slowly peeled my left hand from the strong grip I had on the tree. He then pulled my right hand off the now blood covered tree and began pulling me to the awaiting Patty Wagon by my right ponytail the escorted me in.

The ride to the Police station was long and humiliating. The Patty wagon was cold, dark and smelled like rotten eggs. The ride was bumpy, which made my butt feel as though I had been beaten with a cast iron frying pan. I shivered the entire ride as I looked in fear at the faces of the other kids and the two women who were thrown in that rat trap on wheels prior to us being hurdled in like animals.

The women, who reminded me of Kathy, where smelly and looked as if they had been beat with a baseball bat. I tried not to stare too long for fear they would attack me. But the one woman had muscles larger than any man I'd ever seen in my life. At times, I thought she was actually a man dressed in drag. I felt uneasy as this he-man kept staring me down and

I swore she winked at me several times.

When the patty wagon pulled up to the Police Station muscle woman straightened out her oversized wig, stood up, straightened her skirt and made her way to me.

"Hey there little girl, how about you bunk with me tonight. I will take care of you." She said staring me down.

In my book, her amazon mannerism and fuzzy upper lip confirmed my thoughts of this person actually being a man. This person scared me so much that I regurgitated the pizza I ate earlier that day; Betsy would have been proud. After re-chewing several slices of pepperoni, I took a deep breath, stared boldly at the he-man, then quickly grabbed my stomach as the acid from the reused food caused major pains.

"I'll make sure we hook up." She said as an accompanying Police woman pushed her out.

"The hell if I would ever bunk with you." I said under my breath.

Minutes after Muscle woman and partner were dragged out of the patty wagon it was my turn to leave that rat trap. As I walked through the doors and down the steps, I noticed the mountainous Police station. At that time, I was just waiting to wake up from a nightmare but I knew it was not going to happen.

"How did I get myself into this mess. Dam, I'm no better than Kathy and Douglass." I thought to myself.

"I hate myself." I repeated quietly.

All us kids were taken to a small room where our bodies were searched for weapons, drugs and other things.

"Alright you Negros, what were you thinking taking those barrels?" A white Police officer asked.

Scared that we may suffer the same fate as Bunny we all

remained silent.

"I see none yall have anything to say." He continued.

"Look Niggers, I don't know what you're thinking but being quiet is not helping your situation. And I'm goin' to tell you, if you don't open those mouths, you're goin' to be in so much trouble that not even your dear Dr. King can keep you out of jail." The Police Officer continued.

"Marcus started this hold whole thing." Bunny abruptly said.

"Who the hell is Marcus?" The Police Officer asked.

"The boy who got shot." Bunny continued.

"Yeah, blame it on the dead guy."

"It's true." Niecy said.

"He organized the whole thing." She continued.

"Well, the dead guy may have organized it but yall sure helped him."

"I didn't." I yelled.

"Who are you?" The Police officer asked.

"Kimberly Carter." I said looking at the green painted concrete floor.

"Oh yeah, you were the one hiding behind a tree. What, you chicken out?"

"Yeah" I said as I shook my head in disgust of the situation.

"Then why didn't you just stay home."

"Because I told Marcus I would come."

"Girl, you better learn how to say no before you end up in jail or even worse dead."

"Yes sir." I said as tears began rolling down my cheeks and movies of the Queen choking me to death played endlessly in my head.

"Sir, we just wanted to see what was in the barrels. We didn't hurt anybody." David Moore explained.

"Are yall going to kill us like you did Marcus?" Niecy asked.

"Alright, alright, I'm sick of you kids." The Officer said.

"Officer Harrell, take these kids to the back and get the names of their parents." He continued.

Two hours after our discussion with the Police Officer my mother and Naomi angrily arrived at the Police station. As I sat in the reception area, I saw thunder thighs and Naomi make their way to the reception desk to wait their turn in line.

"May I help you?" The receptionist asked when they approached the receptionist some twenty minutes after arriving.

"Yeah, we're here to pick up Kimberly Carter." The Queen said.

"Oh yeah", the receptionist said.

"Kimberly Carter." she called.

Given the situation I wasn't sure whether it was safer in jail or safer at home with the Queen. As I walked cautiously toward the receptionists I stopped, looked the Queen in her eyes, then took a couple of steps backward. The receptionist, aware of my hesitation, slowly walked toward me to encouraged me to continue. Finally, the moment of truth had arrived.

"Kimberly, are you okay?" The Queen asked with care.

"Yes Ma'am. I'm so sorry Mother."

"I know, I know." She humbly said.

"Did you people take good care of my baby?" The Queen asked.

"Yes, she's fine." The receptionist replied.

"What was wrong with this picture". I said to myself.

I didn't get it, why hadn't she pulled me by my neck, thrown me on the floor and stump all over me. I mean it had been thirty seconds.

"Mrs. Carter, your daughter is really a good kid, please don't be too hard on her. She just needs to learn to say no." Officer Mantle said as he walked up.

"I know officer, I know." The Queen said.

&

Dear Diary,

I really messed up today. The day started out so well. Kevin and I went to his school and had fun with Operation Champ. It was great Diary, I learned so much and Kevin had a blast learning new skills. And Diary, there was tons of food and it was all free. Oh, I ate like a pig.

Well anyway, a boy from my school had some great idea to take the barrels from Mr. And Mrs. Franks' garage and he wanted me to help. At first, I said no, then I let him talk me into helping. After I got there I chickened out and hid behind a tree as the other kids moved the barrels. I can't believe I got myself in a situation like that, I mean all I wanted to do was go home but I didn't want to break a promise.

In the end we all ended up at the Police station. Some of the kids were still there when I left, but they let me come home because I really didn't do anything. Right now, I'm waiting for The Queen to come in and beat me from here to there. So far she hasn't punished me or said anything bad to me. Diary, if you don't hear from me again, you know why.

Well, I guess its time to go. I've been debating whether to tell Kevin, and I think I should, maybe it would help him stay out of this kind of trouble.

Till next time, I hope.

Kim.

Chapter 6

Douglass

Two weeks had passed since that frightening day and surprisingly The Queen had spared my life. As a matter of fact, to this day she has not even mentioned that day. I kept waiting for her to pick up a brick and knock it over my head, but she never did. I really believe she intentionally made me suffer with just the thought of her murdering me, as that would have been the ultimate punishment. But then again, at that time I doubt she had the brains to think of something so devious.

That day I decided to enjoy a totally empty house as the Queen had to work late and Naomi had taken Mae down to the church. So, I invited my Double Dutch group over to practice for the upcoming competition. Me, Darlene, Niecy and Debbie got together on the pavement outside my front door and worked for several hours trying to perfect our routines. Before we knew it, we had been practicing for four hours that unusually warm February day. The sun had just started to set and the street lights had come on before we decided to call it a night. As we packed our jump ropes Douglass appeared out of nowhere dressed in black pants, a black leather vest, a black beret and a blue shirt.

"Hey little sis." He said walking towards the group.

"Why are you dressed like that?" I asked.

"Are you in the Black Panthers?" Darlene asked.

"Yeah, I goda' protect us Negroes from the man."

"What man?" Darlene asked.

"The White Man, you know he'll do anything to make us Niggers look bad."

"My parents say that the Black Panthers are useless and make us look bad." Darlene said.

"Ah, your father wishes he were white." Douglass replied.

"No he doesn't." Darlene said raising her voice.

"Look girl, why don't we get together and talk someday. I'll tell you all about the group that's gonna take over this here United States of America." Douglass said before entering the house.

"I don't know." Darlene said hesitantly as Douglass smiled at her.

"Kim, we're leavin', see you at school on Monday." Niecy said.

"Yeah" Debbie said.

"Okay, bye." I replied.

After Darlene and I finished folding the last jump rope she headed home and I joined Douglass in the kitchen.

"You know, that Darlene needs a little blackening." Douglass said.

"Leave my friend alone." I said as I started making dinner.

"Ah, don't worry, she'll be okay." I said

"Your friend is too white acting. I need to get my hands on her and show her how to be black." Douglass said as the front door opens.

"Douglass, you need to get yourself together." Naomi said as she enters and over hears the conversation.

"You know what, miss religious freak, I'm tired of seeing my mother work all those hours for that white man and barely bringing home a dime. And you, you think scrubbing the white man's floors is a great job. Well I don't. " Douglass stated.

"Cleaning houses is an honest job." Naomi said.

"Look here." He said pointing to his gun.

"This is the only way to make a honest living. You present this to the white man and I guarantee you he will honestly give you every dime in his pocket."

"Oh, get that thing out of this house before somebody gets hurt." Naomi said after laying Mae on the couch then joining me with making dinner.

"I don't have time to spend with you white sympathizers, I have to get over to Eden St."

"For what?" Naomi asked.

"A great Black Panther Party." Douglass said while taking a coat out of the closet and putting it on.

After grabbing a couple pieces of toast Douglass quickly gave me an envelope and ran out the front door. The envelope was addressed to the Queen with the words "*And I will not take this back*" written below her name.

That next evening Naomi, The Queen and I sat in the living room complaining about the sudden turn in the weather when Douglass finally returns home from his Black Panther Party, cloths in disarray, eyes drooping and his skin reaping of marijuana and alcohol. Stumbling in, I noticed that the gun he was sporting the previous day was now missing.

"Didn't you have a gun yesterday?" I asked.

"Leave me alone." Douglass replied.

"Douglass, I'm tired of this. What the Hell have you gotten yourself involved in?" The Queen yelled.

"He joined the Black Panthers." I said.

"The Black Panthers!" The Queen yelled.

"Yeah" I replied.

"So, which group do you belong to, the Industrial Reserve Army or the Criminal Element. Let me guest." The Queen asked.

"Ah, didn't I say leave me alone." Douglass wined.

"I don't give a damn what you said." The Queen said.

"Douglass, I don't think Dr. King likes the Black Panthers." I said.

"Do you think I care what Dr. King thinks. He's not the one who's dodging the draft and it's not him who the Police is beating up on."

"Are you kidding? The Police are always after him. They follow him like a Hawk." I said.

"Let me tell you somethin'. You're a black young male and you will always be a target. Each day you stay in that stupid gang is a day off of your life." Naomi explained.

"No, each day I'm in that gang is a day I'm not dying in some stupid ass war."

"The Black Panthers can't stop you from going to Vietnam?" I yelled in disgust.

"Hey little girl, don't talk to me like that or I'll...."

"You touch my daughter and I will break your neck." The

Queen said as Naomi headed upstairs in disgusts.

Suddenly the room became quiet, except for the ticking of that annoying clock. I was speechless that the Queen actually defended me. Wow, I almost thought she really cared about me.

Upset over the entire conversation Douglass put his head down then headed up stairs. That left me, The Queen and my favorite clock to hate. And of course, I didn't know what to say to the Queen and I don't think she knew what to say to me, so, into separate corners of the house we went.

Chapter 7

An Illegal Act

When I returned home from school that next Monday, I found my mother sitting in the living room staring out of the small window that overlooked the front steps. She looked to have been possessed by some out of world spirit as she paid no attention to me or Mae's crying. To ensure I didn't disturb her I quietly took off my coat, hung it in the small closet near the front door and began tipped toeing upstairs to take care of Mae.

"Hey, where you goin?" She yelled.

"Upstairs to get Mae."

"No, let her cry, you stay down here with me."

"But,,,"

The Queen's facial expression showed that she was in no mood for my defiance, so I passively came back downstairs and sat in the old wooden chair next to her. As she continued to look out of the small window, I continued to sit in the chair swinging my short skinny legs back and forth in sync with the ticking of that stupid clock. Annoyed with the constant swinging the Queen gave me the look of death. Seconds after getting the hint I quickly stopped swinging my legs, leaving that stupid clock to tick without the aid of them.

"One day" I said to myself. "I'm gonna get a hammer and beat that thing into a million pieces." I continued.

After the Queen and I stared silently at each other for a couple of minutes she runs to the door after noticing a strange man approaching.

"Come in" She said to the strange man after opening the front door.

The tall dark-skinned man wearing a long black coat and carrying a black pleather bag enters as ordered. The Queen then points the man toward the steps and he starts towards them.

"Kimberly, come with me." The Queen ordered.

"Wait a minute" I thought to myself.

Why did she think I wanted to see her and this goof ball get it on? Personally, I thought the woman was crazy so I just sat there.

"What did I say?" The Queen said noticing my hesitation.

"Yes Ma'am." I said after I figured she brought in the Calvary to get back at me for getting arrested.

During the trip upstairs I wondered just what could she and this idiot actually do to me. I thought that maybe he was going to hold me down while she grabbed a chain and beat the hell out of me. Then I thought that maybe, just maybe, they were going to knock me out and throw me out a window. At that point neither The Queen nor the stranger gave any clues.

The stranger spoke not one word as he followed the Queen

to her bedroom. Preparing for the beating of my life I slowly made my way into the room after him. The tall dark stranger emptied the contents of his bag on a table next to my mother's bed. Coming to grips with this being my last day on Earth I decided I would not go down without a fight so I prepared myself for the first blow so I could intercept it.

"Take off your pants and get in bed" The stranger ordered.

I wasn't sure whether he was talking to me or the Queen so I cautiously eyed my mother to see her response. Relief came about me when I noticed her slipping off her jeans and panties. She then climbed into bed and laid on her back.

"Hey kid, get over here." The man demanded in a deep voice.

Still not totally convinced that my death sentence had been over turned I cautiously made my way to the impatiently waiting man.

"Open your legs and bend your knees." He demanded of my mother.

"Okay" She responded.

"Here kid sit on her foot until I tell you to get up." The dirty dark-skinned man demanded.

Scared for my life I instantly did as ordered. Seconds afterwards the tall stranger walked to the other side of the bed, sat on The Queen's other foot and proceeded to take some of the tools he pulled from his bag off the nearby table.

After mentally celebrating my stay it finally dawned on me what was about to happen. This would be the last day my worried mother would have to carry a child she had no desires to have and this dark stranger would be the one to rid her of that chore.

The evil looking man, whose name I never knew proceeded

to put on a pair of rubber gloves that had so many holes in them they could have been used as strainers. Before proceeding he took a cigarette out of his pocket, lit it, took a puff then laid it on the table next his tools.

The silent stranger then picked up a tool that resembled a pair of dull medal tongues then commenced his job. Thank God I couldn't see what he was doing because a few minutes into his job and a couple of tools later my mother let out several loud and screeching screams. The look on her face was one of severe pain and anxiety as tears streamed from her eyes.

I couldn't help think that these were not just tears of pain but they were also tears of joy. After focusing on the Queen's scared face for twenty minutes or more I finally got the nerve to look at what that tall stranger was doing. After pulling several dirty instruments from the Queen's body I noticed several bloodstains and clots on the beige colored sheet. Unconcerned, the stranger began packing his tools. At that point I knew that was the end of her latest crisis.

&

Dear Diary,

The date is February 17, 1968, time 3:30 p.m. Well Diary, like usual something out of the ordinary has happened and again it has to do with my mother. She finally had that abortion she's wanted since she found out she was pregnant and I, for some reason, was forced to sit in on it. Diary, I hope I never have to see something like that again. It was degrading, humiliating and dam right disturbing. Diary, that stupid jerk who gave The Queen her wish handled her like a piece of meat. He could care less about the pain he put her in. I swear Diary, if she ever makes me see something like that again, I'm going to get the hell out of there, I swear.

&

My attitude toward the Queen got increasingly worst during the next couple of days. As if it wasn't bad enough to be forced to see her give birth to a live baby it was even worse to see her give birth to a baby she was responsible for killing. And her overall nonchalant attitude about the whole thing had me ready to pick up a brick and knock some sense into her big old head.

As I walked home from school several days after that infamous event my blood started boiling, my head began to hurt and the acids in my stomach multiplied with each passing moment. The thoughts of that awful day had kept me awake every day since. I was tired, I was irritated and I was just plain ole fed up. In a nutshell, I was pissed, I wanted to let the Queen have it, I wanted to tell her ass off and was determined to so. I knew it would be the battle of my life but I was ready to burn her ears with a few choice words.

When I arrived home, I stopped at the front door, took a deep breath, prayed and began turning the doorknob. Upon entering, my first thought was "While, it's so quiet", which was strange because I knew that the Queen had taken the day off from work. "Ok" I said to myself, "I guess she's gone out". I continued to myself as the sounds of the clock resonated in my ears.

Somewhat relieved of a missed opportunity I began walking toward the living room to drop my books off on the worn couch. As I walked toward the couch, I noticed the Queen laying on the floor next to the large window that faced the busy street in front of our house. As I got closer, I noticed blood steadily pouring from her upper legs and that she had become lethargic.

Scare that she was dying I instantly forgot my anger,

grabbed a blanket and put it over her shivering body. "I'll be right back, I'm going next door to use Mrs. Wilson's phone to call the ambulance, ok." I said as I quickly got up.

"Okay." She said as her eyes slowly closed.

"Don't die, please don't die." I said staring at her as she began crying.

Several minutes later Mrs. Wilson and I returned to notice my mother's body completely still. Forgetting all the bad things she had done to us kids, well mainly me, I rushed over and with all my strength turned her on her side. I then put my ear to her nose to see if she was still breathing. I was relieved when I heard her take several shallow breaths.

"Mom, you'll be okay. The ambulance is on its way."

"Delores, don't worry your daughter is taking good care of you." Mrs. Wilson said before my mom gently shook her head in agreement.

Hours later at the Provident Hospital my entire crew of brothers and sisters had gathered in the emergency room waiting area. Exhausted from the extra-long wait most of us had fallen asleep wherever there was room.

"Man, I can't believe my strong loud mother may die. I always thought she was too stubborn to let death come knocking." Beatrice said as she began waking up.

"Yeah, me too", Kathy said.

"She's not going to die." Naomi said.

"How do you know?", I said.

"Because, if God wanted her to go home then he would have taken her by now." Naomi said.

"Naomi that God stuff is crap. How can you believe in something that doesn't exist?" Douglass said in an agitated tone.

"If there was no God then none of us would be here." Naomi said.

"Ah, that's bull. What you should say is, if there was no sex then none of us would be here." Douglass said.

"Hey, you know he has a point." Kathy agreed.

"Yeah, as many times as Mom's been pregnant, I guess she loves her sex." Beatrice said.

"One day she and Freddie were doing it in her bedroom so I peeped at them through the skeleton key hole in the door." Kathy said.

"Well, I have to admit I did the same." Naomi said.

"ORR!!!" Beatrice said as if to imply she performed a shameful sin.

"Oh, I was six or seven at the time." Naomi stated.

"Not me, it was just last year for me." Kathy said.

"You know children, we are in a public hospital." Mrs. Wilson said as she tried to quiet Mae.

"Anyone here for Delores Carter?" A tall stocky white man wearing a white coat said as he made his way into the waiting room.

"Yeah man, where's my mother?" Douglass asked forcefully.

"Boy, what's your name?" The man asked.

"Hey, I'm not your boy."

"A little full of yourself, boy." The man said.

"I goin' to kill you white man." Douglass said upset over the man's attitude and after lunging toward him in anger.

"Douglass, calm down, you're not helping your mother by getting angry." Mrs. Wilson yelled.

"And who are you?" The man asked in a cold manner.

"I'm Mrs. Carter sister." Mrs. Wilson lied.

"Well I guess I can talk to you. Your sister, apparently had an illegal abortion recently and whatever asshole did it caused a lot of damage. She'll be okay, but to society's benefit she will never have another baby. And looking at things this couldn't have come soon enough."

I was shocked at the comments made by this supposedly Doctor. In my eyes this guy was a professional yet his attitude toward Negroes was just as racist as some of the store owners on Pennsylvania Ave. He ruined my faith in all white people. Before that I was under the impression that only the poor whites hated us. Man, what a wake-up call.

"Hey white man, you say another racist thing and I'm going to introduce my gun to your heart, is that clear?" Douglass said.

"Dr. when can we see her?" Naomi asked ignoring Douglass' comment.

"You can go in now, she's in room ten. I'll get a nurse to escort you to make sure you folks don't do something you shouldn't."

Chapter 8

The Test

The events of the previous week were embarrassing and damn right upsetting. I hated the Queen for forcing me to witness such a horrible act. In my book, she deserved to lose her natural right to bear more children. Just think about it, anybody, just anybody, who would force their young daughter to see something like that should lose the rights to all their children.

My brothers and sisters performed a bonding act during the Queen's stay in the hospital. Kathy and Douglass spent most their time at home helping Naomi take care of us younger kids. Kathy even made dinner several days in a row and helped me take care of Mae so I could study for the upcoming test. Douglass graciously walked Kevin to and from school each day and made sure he got his homework done. At one point, I could have sworn we were transformed into a Ghetto Cleaver family.

Though the Queen was somewhat quiet and reframed from

speaking when she returned home it didn't take long for that to change. Within an hour she didn't hesitate to order me around. "Clean this, clean that, cook me this, cook me that, why is the baby crying, the hell if you are going to take a break and study." That's all I heard for the first four hours. At one point, I wanted to stuff a few cotton balls in that awful mouth to shut it up.

After eight hours of bossing me around she falls asleep on the couch. It was a pleasant and calming site. That was one of those moments when I wished I could have bottled what ever made her fall asleep and have it ready to put in her coffee the next time she got on my nerves. Well anyway, I knew I had to take advantage of that moment and sneak in a couple of hours of studying, after all the test was just days away.

After gathering my books and carefully arranging then on a small table in the back room of the basement I was mentally ready for a long study session. So, after sitting down and opening the first book I began reading a chapter on The War of 1812. But, within several minutes the text in the book grew larger and larger; I just couldn't stop the growth. No matter how hard I tried it just kept growing. The next thing I knew that same text had become blurry. An hour later, same thing, two hours later same thing finally by the third hour I just gave up, it just wasn't going to happen. So down went the head and off to dream land I went.

&

Studying was pretty much non-existent that week before the test and it weighed heavily on my mind as the test date was now just one day away. Feeling guilty for slacking and breaking a promise to Mr. Parkinston to study every night before the test I found myself a nervous wreck. My concentration was non-existent; my memory was shot and my temper was short. After her first day home, the Queen didn't bother sensing my anger.

Finally, the test day arrived. Mentally I was still shot. During the bus ride from my home in Western Baltimore City to The Western High School in Northwest Baltimore my stress levels quadrupled and quadrupled and triple quadrupled. I just couldn't believe that some stupid idiot in some stupid office somewhere thought that a ninth grader would know Calculus and every damn battle in the Civil War. Just how could a ninth grader know all that Regional Geography, I mean hell, before studying for that sorry test I had never even heard of some of those places. Gosh if it weren't for Mr. Parkinston, I swear I would have never known all that stuff, especially since my sorry ass school failed to educate me.

I arrived at Western High School at 7:30 that morning, one half hour before the official test starting time. As I disembarked the bus, I notice more than 40 black kids sitting on the stone planters outside the school's front door. Trying to size up the competition I panned the many faces, contemplating the depth of their knowledge, but to no surprise that was an impossible task. Stress had turned my mind into mush leaving me searching my many brains cells for the few that were still working.

Fifteen minutes after arriving at the test site the number of test takers had doubled in size which exponentially increased my stress levels. The entire situation had my hands sweating large drops of purified water, had my left eye uncontrollably twitching and gave me an incredible urge to go to the bedroom.

"Students." A tall white man said approaching the crowd.

"Line up at the station in which you find the first letter of your last name. Once you reach the table, give the official your full name and your current school. The official will then give you a piece of paper with the classroom in which you are to go, along with the name of the test administrator. You are then to proceed to your classroom and sit at the desk in which your name tag sits. There are signs directing you to each of the classrooms, so follow them and you won't get lost." The man continued before taking several deep coughs.

Five minutes later I found myself sitting in a classroom of twelve other black girls. For some reason the girls were separated from the boys. At the time, I thought they really didn't think us girls could compete against the boys so they wanted to instantly separate our test in an effort to not waste time grading them. And that made me mad. Just the thought of those white people fixing the results calmed my spasms, stopped my sweating and relieved my urges to go to the bathroom. I now had another reason for wanting to do well on the test.

Suddenly my concentration returned and connections between all my brain cells were re-established. I could once again focus and was patiently waiting for the test to begin. I was calm, unlike most of the other girls in the room. Several of them impatiently skimmed their notes, hands shaking as they rattled through the pages.

"Oh no, here comes the tester. He doesn't look too nice with his mean mug and three-piece blue plaid suit." I said to myself.

His dominate presence seem to frazzle the other girls in the room, but I was as calm as a leaf on a still summer day.

"Thank you" I said after the plaid suit man handed me the test booklet, test sheet and a number 2 pencil.

"Well Kid" I said to myself "This is it, good luck." I

continued.

Before I knew it, the four-hour exam was over. I couldn't believe it; I knew I had a better than average chance of winning that scholarship. I answered every question and even had a chance to review my answers. In the back of my mind I knew the only reason I did a great job was because of Mr. Parkinston. I knew that even if I didn't get the scholarship, it didn't matter because nobody, just nobody, could take away all the stuff I learned to prepare for the test.

Chapter 9

A Gift Stolen

Well, as I expected, it didn't take long for life at my humble abode to get back to normal. The Queen was swearing and cursing again; Kathy's desire to work in the world's oldest profession continued and the rest of the, quote family, unquote were going about their daily business. But, despite the dysfunctional behavior of the odd crew I had hoped that the next week would pull them together to celebrate my fourteenth birthday.

At the time, I really thought things would be different. Usually my birthday would come and go totally unnoticed, but this year two of my darling siblings briefly made mention of the upcoming day. A couple of days earlier Kathy asked me what I wanted and she actually seemed a little excited. But Kathy didn't surprise me as much as Douglass.

Out of the blue he approached me and said "So kid you're about to turn fourteen. It's about time you started doing things teenagers do, you get my drift." I didn't have the foggiest idea what he meant but I agreed and that brought a large smile on his somewhat plain pimpled filled face.

Two days later I discovered the answer to his question. After my fifth check for the mail I decided to raid the refrigerator for something to drink. As I approached the kitchen, I saw Douglass and three strange looking characters sitting around the dilapidated kitchen table.

As I got closer, I noticed them passing around something on a small piece of paper and something that looked like a straw. I froze and just stood in the doorway trying to decide whether to continue or just wait until some force of nature released my feet from its glued hold on the old wooden floor. Suddenly, after releasing the strong hold of my right foot from the floor I noticed one of the guys taking the straw, slowly put one end up his nose, leaned toward the paper and begin sniffing the white powdery substance.

Seconds later he took a deep breath, leaned back in the chair and took a deep sniff. As he attempted to breath normally a gush of blood flowed rapidly out of the nostril in which he had just removed the straw. He then took his right hand and wiped away what blood he could. Unaffected by his bleeding episode, the guy replaced the straw and continued sniffing the powdery substance. About three minutes later he passed the blood covered straw and the paper to the next guy who in turn followed suit.

I was shocked, I always knew Douglass was into that stuff but I never thought he would have the nerve to do that mess in his own mother's home. Just to look at this made me sick to my stomach. I was ready to run to the upstairs bathroom and throw up when Douglass spotted me.

"Hey sis, come here."

Though I heard his request my brain failed to comprehend it. I just stood as numbness invaded my body from the tips of my toes to the top of my forehead. I couldn't seem to breathe for it seem as though I had no lungs. My eyes focused yet fogged, could only interpret the shadow outlines of my big brother and his drugged-up friends. In a nutshell, I was defeated. All of a sudden Douglass gets out of his chair and walks toward me.

"Hey kid, what's wrong, you act like you've just seen a ghost." He calmly said as he hugged me and somehow got my feet moving towards the table.

"Now, come here, I want you to meet a few friends. This is old man Joe. We're best best buddies." He said pointing to the nose bleeder whose nose had now started bleeding like Niagara Falls.

"And these two jack asses are Ken Ben and Rocko." Pointing to the two guys who had just passed out on the very table we ate our meals on every day.

"Have a seat, have a seat." Douglass happily said as he pulled out the chair next to the chair he was just sitting on.

"Kim, you know we're been brother and sister for what, fourteen years now."

"Yeah" I reluctantly said.

"And it's been a great fourteen years, hasn't it?"

"Yeah, I guess so."

"And as you know, I would never do anything to hurt you, now would I."

"Well, I guess not."

Douglass' eyes brightened when he noticed a very faint smile come about my normally emotionless face. Though I thought Douglass believed I was happy to join his nose bleeding session my thoughts were actually on getting the hell out of there and leaving in the same manner in which I came.

"So Kim, just how much money do you have?" He asked as

he backed away from my chair.

"I don't know, I haven't looked at my bank book lately." I lied.

"Oh I see. Well kid, I tell you what. Since we've been brother and sister for so long, I'm going to cut you a break." He said as if he were doing me a favor.

He then dug into the left pocket of his brown sweat jacket and pulled out a plastic bag of white stuff and another small straw. After walking back to the table, pushing my chair in as he moved along, he carefully opened the bag and poured the contents on a plate he retrieved from a pile of dirty dishes. Seconds after using a razor blade to push the white powder into small piles he handed me the straw and waited as I looked at him like he was crazy.

After finally realizing I had no idea and no desires to learn how to use that stuff he moved closer, put his right arm around my left shoulder and picked up the straw.

"Here sis I'm goin' to teach you how to get the best feeling in the world. This stuff can become your very best friend. It can give you a feeling like no human could ever give you." He confidently remarked as he put the straw in my right hand.

"Put it halfway up your nose." He softly ordered.

Though his request was disturbing and I wanted to tell Douglass to go to hell I was reluctant to disappoint my oldest brother. So, I took one short sniff of the powdery stuff and got a little up my nose before throwing the straw on the floor. Thirty minutes later my head was spinning and my body felt as light as air. The feeling was so overwhelming that I could barely hold my balance to prevent from leaning to either side and ending up on the kitchen floor.

Coming to grips with the ills of my action I knew it was

time to leave the situation I had created. As I attempted to stand and make my way upstairs, I looked to the right to see the bleeder's nose had stopped spilling life preserving liquids. He was just sitting there, giving me the most uncomfortable look, but I didn't think much of it.

My inability to control my movements became evident as I stumbled from the kitchen to the stairs leading to the bedrooms above. Having knocked over a lamp and everything else on the same table it had sat I wondered just how I was supposed to navigate the long and narrow stairs. The steps, that normally weren't a challenge even for a two-year old, had taken on the characteristics of the Mighty Grand Canyon.

Looking at the stairs I couldn't figure out how I was supposed to get my body to navigate them. Unfortunately, it had become evident that I needed Olympic training to accomplish the task at hand. But, since something didn't seem right with that bleeder, I knew I had to escape the evil ways of Douglass and of the crazed looking bleeder. But I didn't have the strength to climb the massive structure. I just wanted to cry.

"Kim, Kim my baby sister." Douglass said approaching, bleeder in tow.

"What?" I replied upset over the situation.

"Now, there's no need to get upset." Douglass said.

"Leave me alone, I should have never let you talk me into taking that stuff!"

"Oh, it's not that bad, little sis. You'll thank me for this one day." Douglass said.

"Go to hell!"

"Woo, where did that come from. My little sister would

never say something like that to her great older brother." Douglass said in shock.

"Well, when her great older brother treats his little sister like one of his junky friends they do." I replied.

"You know life's too short to wait for your first high. You should appreciate the fact that I gave you yours for free."

"Leave me alone!" I said attempting to move my right foot from the first floor to the first step of the massive staircase.

After struggling for several seconds, I was still unable to accomplish my goal so I simply gave up, turned around and sat on that very step. As reality set in the thought of spending the next couple of hours with a brother I now hated, a bleeding ugly scare faced junkie and two goof-balls who still haven't lifted their nappy heads off our kitchen table scared the hell out of me.

With each passing moment, the fear became more and more overwhelming leading me to uncontrollably crying. First it began as just a few drops of tears but ended with the faucets wide opened.

"Please God let The Queen come home, please." I mumbled in disbelief to myself.

"Please!"

"Little Girl, I'll carry you upstairs." The Bleeder said.

"I don't want you to touch me." I said in an angry voice.

"Ah, I'm not gonna' hurt you." The bleeder responded.

"Leave me alone!" I screamed in an irritate voice.

"Kim, he won't hurt you. I promise." Douglass said.

"I don't like him. Get him away from me." I screamed.

"I won't let him hurt you, you're my sister." Douglass continued.

I looked into Douglass' eyes for several seconds then decided to trust him and give the bleeder a chance.

"Okay." I calmly said to the bleeder.

After peeling several dried spots of blood from just below his nose and wiping his blood-stained hand on the back of his pants he put on the biggest happiest smile. He then carefully lifted me to his right shoulder and carried me to the door of my room. From the second he picked me up to the second we arrived at the top of the stairs that uneasy feeling I felt earlier multiplied several times over.

"Put me down." I demanded.

"But I haven't taken you to your bed yet." He said.

"I don't care. I can walk by myself." I said wiggling.

"Why, it's only a few more feet?" He attempted to explain.

"So, I can walk." I replied in a nasty tone.

"Kim, why are you so hard on my man. He won't hurt you I promise." Douglass said as he reached the top of the steps.

"No, let me down." I insisted as the blood once again began pouring from the bleeder's nose and onto my left arm.

"Okay" He said before carefully setting me down to my feet.

Eager to get the hell away from this horrid game I tried with all my strength to move my feet through the doorway and away from my brother and his partner in crime. But my body had other ideas as the dizziness and clumsiness returned with a vengeance. No sooner than my feet hit the floor than the room began spinning.

"Little girl, I got you." The Bleeder said catching me.

To prevent me from banging my head on the floor the bleeder picked he gracefully then laid me on my bed. He sat next to me with those scary eyes staring at me.

"You know you're a very pretty young girl." He said stroking my hair.

"I bet you're innocent, aren't you? I like girls that way, it gives me a challenge and it feels so good." He continued staring at me.

"You know today should be your day of first. First your brother gave you your first high and now it's time for your first man."

"Leave me alone!" I scream as I began kicking.

"Ah Kim, it won't hurt. Kathy does it all the time and she's okay." Douglass said.

"No, I don't want to do it." I screamed attempting to get up and wondering why my own brother would side with the likes of the bleeder.

I guess it wasn't enough that he made me take that stuff, but now he wanted me to do it with some junky who had the looks of the flying cow in the Wizard of OZ.

Douglass, convinced he had earned his friend a sex session, leaves me and the horny bleeder alone in close quarters. As the bleeder reaches toward my lame body and attempts to take off my pants I screamed to the top of my lungs. Minutes passed and no one came, not even my big brother. When the bleeder managed to take off my pants my screams got louder and more intense. He then covered my mouth and laid on top on me.

Struggling to push him off my body I finally became so numb that I had no fight left in my soul. My future was now in the hands of a man capable of filling our kitchen sink with a boat load of blood.

An hour later I woke up realizing that I had passed out during the bleeder's raid on my body. At the time, I felt as though I lost something special but all I remembered was that that Nigger laid on top of me and rubbed his dirty dick against my skinny brown legs. I felt damn right filthy.

As the weeks rolled by the thoughts of that day made me sick to my stomach. The more I thought about it the sicker I got. There were times I threw up just thinking about it. I hated Douglass for allowing some jack-ass to do that to me. I felt that he and that jack-ass robed me of my most precious gift from God. And that jack-ass was now running the streets of Baltimore robbing other girls of their gift.

I wanted to tell somebody about that horrible incident, but I was ashamed. I was so ashamed that I decided not to tell anybody and that included my best friend. I just couldn't bring myself to recreate that horrid crime. I just wanted to block it out and pretend it never happened. Though I knew it was going to be hard I also wanted to pretend I had no older brother.

&

It was now the day I had been waiting for, my birthday. I was officially fourteen years old. For some reason, I thought that I would feel different but I didn't. Of course, it had only been a few hours, but I thought I would feel more grown up the second I turned fourteen.

I hoped that day would be celebrated by the entire family. In the past, it seemed as though the only people who celebrated my birthday were me and Kevin. Well, that wasn't exactly true. Mr. Parkinston always gave me a box of candy and a card with money. This year he gave me a bright red bicycle and twenty dollars and instructed me to put the money in the bank for my future. At the time, I thought he felt sorry for me, especially after finding out that my mother always forgot my birthday. For some reason, that year, I had a gut feeling things would be different with my family.

To my surprise, my instincts were right. After dinner Kathy gave me a chocolate cake with fourteen candles lit as bright as the day.

"Happy birthday to a swell kid." She said as she placed the cake in front of me.

"Oh goodness, look whose tryin' to be nice, the family slut." Douglass said.

"Oh go to hell, you're just jealous that I have a nice bone in my body and you don't."

"Yeah right, you just want somethin' from her, you know it, I know it and Kim knows it."

"I wish you damn children would shut those fuckin' mouths up." The Queen said as she lit her fifth cigarette of the hour.

All the yelling and screaming came to a screeching halt and remained so for quite some time. Then finally my precious little brother Kevin headed up-stairs.

"Kevin where are you goin'?" I yelled.

"I'll be right back, I'm goin' to get something." He replied.

"Well hurry up, I have a date." The Queen ordered.

"You forever have a date, if you would stay home more maybe you wouldn't get knocked up some much." Beatrice said in a low voice.

"I'm goin' to ignored that." The Queen replied.

Beatrice could care less about the Queen and her smart responses. The Queen, as well as the rest of the family, were used to Beatrice's constant belittling of the family and how we lived. Whether it was the old furniture, the way we dressed or what we did, nothing seemed to please her. And don't let her get started on the Queen, who was the target of most of her complaints. Beatrice had it in for the Queen, blaming her for the way we lived. It really wasn't so bad, I mean we didn't have much but we did have a somewhat normal life, in our own little way, of course.

As the minutes passed on that loud ticking clock the friction between Beatrice and the Queen grew intense. As the clock struck 4:30 it resonated an eerie annoying sound and the Queen finished her fifth cigarette. Frustrated with the situation the Queen decides it was time for her to leave, as she felt that she was about to do something she would regret. After stuffing five dollars in my right hand and giving me a very faint "Happy birthday" she picked up her bag and headed out the back door.

"I'm sorry I can't give you more." Kathy said handing me a one-dollar bill as the door closes behind the Queen.

"Well I can." Douglass confidently said as he pulled out a two-inch-thick roll of bills, opened it and began peeling off fives.

After sliding four fives in front of me he noticed the next bill was a hundred so he quickly stopped and proceeded to re-roll the bills, which was now sandwiched by a hundred and a fifty.

"Why are you goin' to give that girl money you got from selling dope?" Kathy said.

"Don't worry about that." Douglass said before leaving the room.

"Well kid, see you later, I have things to do." Kathy remarked as she slipped through the back door.

"Here you go Kim. I love you little sister." Beatrice said handing me a couple of dollars.

"Thanks Beatrice. I love you also." I said before giving her a hug.

Suddenly finding myself with twenty-eight dollars I started thinking that despite my sisters and brothers yelling and despite that very few of my family members stayed for cake things went pretty well. I mean it was great, this was the first time in months the entire family gathered for dinner, and it was all because of my birthday.

As I collected the money and Beatrice and I blew out the candles on the cake Kevin returned carrying a small red box wrapped in a huge white bow. He slowly walks toward me displaying the largest smile I had ever seen on a kid his size. Just to see the sparkling glitter in his eyes and the blush in his cheeks was enough present for me.

"Happy birthday" he said as he handed me the card and box.

"Thank you." I said as I gently took them then laying the box on the table before proceeding to open the envelope.

When I removed the content of the envelope, I found a handmade Birthday card. On the front was a pretty good drawing of a small boy and an older girl fishing on a pier. It wasn't a Picasso but it was pretty darn good. The card was made from pink construction paper and had several green and yellow flowers drawn on the front. The caption, written in a pretty orange crayon, read

Something Special for A Special Sister
with Love from Kevin

On the inside of the card were three lines written in very large print, they read.

HAPPY BIRTHDAY
WITH ALL MY HEART
TO THE BEST SISTER IN THE WORLD!

When I finally opened the box, I pulled out a heart shaped locket with a picture of Kevin and I fishing on the piers of downtown Baltimore. That picture was taken by his father when he took the two of us fishing one-day last year. I couldn't help from crying as I thought about all the work he had put into my gift. I wanted to give him a tight bear hug and that I did.

&

Dear Diary,

This has been the most perfect birthday, it was great. The entire family, that is everybody except Naomi, got together and celebrated my birthday. I was so thrilled. Let me tell you what I got. Mom, Kathy, Douglass and Beatrice together gave me $28.00. Mr. Parkinston, Diary listen to this. Mr. Parkinston gave me a bright red bicycle and money. The Queen wasn't too thrilled but she let me keep them anyway, I couldn't believe that. I still wonder how he knew I always wanted a bike.

But you know what, the very best gift of all came from Kevin. Along with a card, that I'll treasure for life, he gave me a locket. Apparently, he had been working for months to earn money to buy it. Diary I wish you could have been there; it was so nice.

My entire family, in their own little way showed their love for me. That is everybody except Naomi. Don't get me wrong I have nothing against going to church and worshipping God but she spends too much time doing it. It's as if he's the only person in the world and the rest of us are just grains of sand in a Sea of desert. I guess I really shouldn't complain but that's the way I feel.

Kim

Chapter 10

Signs of the Times

That next Saturday couldn't have come soon enough. Sleeping until I felt like getting up, looking at t.v. and making a pig out of myself were all on the agenda. My schedule was all planned, I would get up around 10:00, make me and Kevin a nice hot breakfast, turn on the t.v. and lounge around in my night clothes for the rest of the day.

My plan started out well when I somehow managed to sleep until 11:00 and I only woke up then because Kevin came in my room and jumped on the bed. Even though I could have slept for another hour I got up, washed up then headed downstairs. An hour later Kevin and I had completed a large breakfast of pancakes, sausage and eggs and was then heading to the t.v. to watch Saturday morning cartoons. Then out of the blue The Queen rushes downstairs and into the living room.

"Kimberly get dressed." The Queen said.

"Why?" I asked.

"Don't question me, I said get dressed."

"Yes Ma'am."

"Mommy, are you and Kim going someplace?" Kevin asked as I headed for the stairs.

"Yes dear, I'm taking Kim with me to buy a new kitchen table."

"Oh, can I go?" Kevin asked.

"If you want." The Queen replied.

&

My mother, Kevin and I made our way to the shopping district just up the street on Pennsylvania Ave. Along with Mr. Parkinston's store there were three furniture stores. The first store, "Inner City World Furniture" was owned by a Jewish couple, Lbieb Shipiro and his wife Madeline and carried furniture from all parts of the world. But despite the large selection this store was disliked by most residents because they felt the attitude of Lbieb left a lot to be desired as he repeatedly disparaged the Negro patrons. Some of the stronger willed Negroes claimed they saw the nicer side of Lbieb and that's why he remained in business.

Regardless of Lbieb's reputation the Queen decided that The Inner City World Furniture store was the best place to begin our search for that perfect set. As we entered, Lbieb walked toward the door, noticed us and hardly spoke a word as he headed toward the back of the store. But his lack of business acumen didn't discourage the Queen from browsing the many items within the store.

"Good morning." The Queen said as she walked to the back of the store and approached Mr. Shipiro.

"Yeah" He said in a rush to get away from the Queen as if she had the plague.

"Well, he could at least have stopped and waited on us." The Queen said brushing off Mr. Shipiro's actions.

Kevin and I joined the Queen at the back of the store and shook our heads in agreement. Disregarding Lbieb's lack of manners the Queen continued browsing the many table and chair sets before noticing several sets that would fit perfectly in our small dim kitchen. After panning the group of sets my eyes focused on a set composed of a green table top with steel legs. It was about seven feet long and about three feet wide and seem to be just large enough to sit our large family. The set came with eight chairs whose cushion seats matched the table's top. Kevin, after noticing my fixation with the set, climbed into one of the chairs and motioned as if eating a hearty Thanksgiving dinner. The Queen and I were tickled at the young actor's performance but that was more than I could say for Lbieb who angrily approached our trio immediately upon noticing.

"What is he doing, get him out of my chair." Mr. Shipiro said in an angry tone.

"He's not harming anything" I said.

"Right now he isn't, but later he will be." Mr. Shipiro replied in a nasty tone.

"Mr. Shipiro I can guarantee you that my son will not damage your precious little chair."

"You cannot guarantee anything, you Niggers have no control of your herd of children."

"Excuse me." The Queen said putting her left hand on her left hip.

"That is correct, why don't you just go to Mondawmin or someplace else. I don't want your money."

"What, but we didn't do anything." I said.

"Kimberly, what he's really saying is that he doesn't think we have the money for his sorry ass table and chairs." The Queen said.

"Kevin let's go." She continued as the three of us headed toward the door. The Queen then stops, turns around, and takes a hand full of cash out of her pocket.

"You see this Jew Man, this is more than enough to pay for your stupid-ass table and chairs." She said before pushing us out the door.

"Mom maybe we should go to Montgomery Ward." I said as the Queen stopped to straighten out that awful blue scarf she keeps sporting on her head.

"No." She Said without hesitation.

"I shouldn't have to take the bus to buy a dinette set." She continued as she grabs Kevin by the arm and begins to walk toward several other furniture stores.

The incident at The Inner City World Furniture Store seem to have no effect on the Queen, she just simply returned her money to her purse and walked two blocks to the "Our Faith Furniture" store. That furniture store was owned by a young black family, the Mores, who years prior moved from the Druid Heights area to a county suburb called Randallstown. At one point the family attended the same church as Naomi but now attends one of the large churches on McCullon Street.

"Good morning cutie, no I guess I should say good afternoon." A short stocky balding man said as we entered the store and noticing the time on a nearby clock reading 12:45.

"Good afternoon." The Queen said.

"Tell me lovely lady how can I help you this fine day." He said putting his right arm around The Queen's waist. But this act of affection didn't sit well with the Queen as she immediately knocked him in his oversized gut with her left elbow then stare angrily at him.

"Oh, I'm sorry, I'm just a touchy, feely type of guy." He said retracting his arm.

"Look we are here to purchase a breakfast table and chair set." The Queen said in an angry tone.

"No problem Honey. Come with me." He said as he escorted us to a section in the back of the store where numerous sets were located. "Now here we have a great variety of sets.

"There're only five." I said.

"Oh, you're a smart one." Mr. Mores said as The Queen chuckled in agreement.

"Each one of these sets is perfect for a fine family like yours and our prices are better than any store in this entire city. If you even look in another store you will be doing yourself an injustice." He said.

"I'm not sure I like any of these." The Queen said as she looked carefully at a couple of sets.

"Now Baby, you know I would never steer you to buy something you didn't want." Mr. Mores said.

"And how do I know that?" The Queen said rolling her head.

"Because it's me, God fairing, honest and Negro."

"So." The Queen said.

"Mom, I like this one. It's the same as the one in the other store just a different color." I said.

"Yeah Honey" Mr. Mores said as if he discovered the set. "This set is perfect for your lovely family. It's strong, modern and is priced just right for you at only one hundred and fifty dollars." He continued.

"I agree with you Kimberly. It is the same as the other one." The Queen said as she walked around the set and as I took a deep sigh of relief when she didn't scold me for giving my opinion. The set mesmerized the Queen for fifteen minutes as she sat in each chair, getting a viewpoint from every position before moving on to the next chair.

"Baby, I just knew you would like this great set. You look so sexy at it." Mr. Mores said.

"Will you stop calling my mother Honey and Baby." Kevin yelled realizing that every guy in the past whose called her those names ended up hurting her feelings.

"Well little man, someday you'll call some fine ladies sexy names like that."

"No I won't." Kevin angrily yelled as he stumped his right foot on the floor.

"We'll see." Mr. Mores said.

"Alright, we will take this one." The Queen said standing up. "But, if you don't watch your fresh mouth I will take my fist and stuff it down your fat throat." She continued.

"Okay, okay I see I'm cornered. (Pause) Ah right, let's sit at your table and chair set and sign the papers."

The two of them sat next to each other on one side of the table then Mr. Mores began writing on a form attached to the clipboard he was carrying.

"Alright." He said. "With taxes and other fees, the total comes to two hundred and fifty-three dollars and twenty cents" He finished.

"What do you mean two hundred and fifty-three dollars, you said it cost one hundred and fifty dollars. Ain't that much taxes in the world." I said.

"Well, you know you can pay my price and get a great set or not have a set at all." Mr. Mores said in a nasty tone.

As my mother pondered over the man's comments I waited patiently for her response.

"I think we should take our money someplace else. He's trying to rip us off." I blurted out loud as I shivered in my shoes in fear of being reprimanded in public for speaking up.

The Queen looked angrily at me then turned her head to face our con-artist salesman.

"You know what baldy, my fourteen-year-old daughter has more common sense than you ever will have. You may sucker some of these uneducated Negroes into buying your over-priced scrap but I will never give you a dime." The Queen yelled.

"Hey, look I'll make a deal with you. I will give you the set for a hundred- and fifty-dollars cash today and you can finance one hundred and twenty at an interest rate of twenty five percent for four years." The man begged as if we were stupid or something.

"Mother, don't do it because then you will pay over three hundred dollars. I say let's go to Laura's Furniture store." I said getting angry.

"You're right Kim." My mother said standing up.

"Good Bye, you fresh stupid little Negro." She said as the three of us headed for the door.

The shopping day was not going as The Queen had planned. With each stop her frustrations grew as she was shocked at the manner in which each of the store owners treated us. But despite her disappointments she charged to the next store as if she were a member of the Calvary charging into Little Big Horn.

After the first two defeats, we entered Laura's Furniture store where we were treated like the President of the United States. Several minutes and one hundred and twenty-five dollars later we emerged victoriously from the furniture store proud owners of a set just like the one in the other two stores but just blue.

Chapter 11

Revelation

Dear Diary,

Date March 3, 1968, time 5:14 p.m. Diary, I've been doing a lot of thinking lately, mostly about prejudice and racism. I don't know, every since that incident in the hospital and the fight between The Queen and Mr. Shipiro I started to realize that there's another world out there. Diary, I realize that everybody's not black and everybody's not poor. I guess I always knew it but it just didn't hit me like it has recently. I figure it's because I really didn't want to see it. I wanted to believe that everybody got along and that color was a figment of some rebel's imagination. Now I know what all the rioting in the country is all about and what Dr. King is fighting for, to end the crazy attitudes and warped thinking of white America.

I guess I should include well off black folks because after speaking with Mr. Parkinston yesterday he made me realize that some Negroes with money treat us just as badly as some whites. From what he said there are people who will never give a poor person any respect. But he also said there are lots of people, both black and white, who are fighting hard to help us one day live a better life. With all this sometimes I wonder why I'm killing myself trying to be good, it's a big waste of time. Diary I think to myself that even if I get the scholarship there're no guarantees I will get out of this Hell hole. I don't know, sometimes I wonder if Marcus isn't in a better place.

Well Diary it's that time again I must say goodbye. I'll talk with later. Till then.

Love Kim

"Gosh you still write in that stupid thing." Kathy said as she runs into the bedroom.

"Yeah, now leave me alone." I replied irritated.

"Give me that damn book." Kathy screamed as she snatches the diary from my hands.

My quiet session with my best friend had quickly turn into a fight with a girl I had absolutely no chance of beating, but what the heck I gave it a try. Moments after starting our screaming, fist fighting and scratching session it slowly turned into a silly, funny tug of war.

I couldn't believe it; Kathy and I were actually enjoying each other's company. Though we were treating my best friend like a hundred-dollar bill it didn't seem to bother me. By the end of the struggle I had possession of my Diary and Kathy was laying on the floor laughing up a storm.

"I'm sorry." She said between laughs.

"Apology accepted." I said smiling.

The room all of a sudden got quiet and stayed that way for several minutes. Not sure what to make of the deafening quiet. I looked at Kathy, trying to figure out what she was thinking. With Kathy it could have been anything so I let her be as I locked the Diary and put in on top of the nearby dresser. Kathy slowly sat up while staring at me. I had a feeling she wanted to say something but nothing. Then finally it came.

"I envy you." She said in a serious tone.

"Why?"

"Well, I guess because you're so young, you still have time to make up for any stupid things you've done."

"I don't get it."

"Look, a lot of people around here have written me off and I deserved it. I've already fucked up my life, I've been arrested a good ten times, I've sold myself to God knows how many men (Pause) and I don't even want to think about what I haven't done in school, which pretty much amounts to nothing. But you, you are already trying to get out of this rat house."

"Just because you've had a rocky pass, that doesn't mean you can't get out of this place. You could go back to school, so what if you'll be behind. If you're really serious it won't matter. After you graduate you could get a decent job and move to the county. There's always a way out."

"You're right, maybe I'll take the advice of my younger sister. Shit, she has more since than me." Kathy said as she wiped a few tears from her eyes.

"Kimberly!" My mother said barging into the room.

"Yes Ma'am." I answered.

"Why didn't you do those damn dishes?"

"I'm sorry, I'll do them right now." I said before opening my dresser draw to put my diary away.

"Give me that thing." She angrily said.

"What?"

"Give me that damn book." She said even more angry.

Hesitant, I handed my best friend to a woman who was not

to be trusted. As she took it, she looked me in the eyes, opened it and began tearing pages into hundreds of tiny pieces. Attempting to grab her right hand to prevent it from tearing more pages she quickly pushed me aside and completed tearing the rest of the pages. By the time she was done my best friend was laying all over my bedroom floor and the tears had clouded my vision to the point I failed to comprehend the damage.

"That should teach you not to do your chores." The Queen said.

"Bitch." Kathy said.

"Don't worry." Kathy continued.

"Her turn will come." She said as the Queen headed for the door.

"Gosh, I hate you" I yelled.

"Excuse me." The Queen said placing her left arm on her left hip then turning to face me.

"You heard me, I hate you. I wish I had a father because I would go and live with him."

"And why in the hell do you think your father would want you?"

"Just because."

"Well I have news for you your father knows where to find you and he hasn't come to get you yet."

"What?" I said in shock.

"Oh yeah, your great Mr. Parkinston is your humble daddy and he could care less about taking you to live with him." She emphasized.

"Huh?" I replied shockingly.

"Huh" She remarked sarcastically before leaving the room.

Chapter 12

Explosion of a city

Thursday April 4, 1968

7:00 p.m.

Unlike most days, our house was full of activity this sunny and bright day. Pretty much every member of the family had gathered in the living room to do whatever they wanted. To some miracle, the Queen was playing on the floor with Mae and actually seem to be enjoying herself. This was the first time in months that the Queen didn't mind spending time with us.

Naomi and Kathy seem to bond by engaging in endless conversations about different things and as usual Kevin and I were hanging together playing Crazy Eights on the small coffee table next to the couch where Kathy and Naomi were sitting. Beatrice, on the other hand, was sitting solo next to an old record player listening to endless Tom Jones' records.

"Beatrice, you know black people make music too." Kathy said.

"And?" Beatrice replied.

"What she means is that we're tired of listening to all that white music." Kevin said as he got up and walked over to the record player. Kevin, insensitive to Beatrice' feelings, takes the needle off the playing record and removes the record from the player. Against Beatrice's protest Kevin retrieves a record from the large stack next to the record player and puts it on. Suddenly, the music starts and the entire family, including Beatrice, began dancing as Kevin started singing and emulating the great James Brown performing his famous song "I feel good".

Kevin, as young as he was, had the most energetic interpretation of the "King of Soul". The song had him spinning on the floor, singing into a pencil and shaking his fifteen-inch waist. By the time the song ended Kevin had fallen to his knees, leaned back and had raised his left hand as he sang into the pencil. Oh, it was great to see the entire family having a good time; it gave me hope that our dysfunctional group may one day actually earn the title of family.

April 4, 1968

That night seem to have the makings of a fun evening. The singing, the dancing, the talking and the goofing around took control of our household for hours without us even realizing it. It was the first time that us kids were able to joke around with the Queen and her not ordering us to go out back to get a switch off the large Oak tree in the back yard. At one time the Queen and I were able to laugh about some of the stupid things we both did.

"Oh, those son-of-a-bitches" Douglass yelled as he stormed into the house.

"Douglass, what's wrong with you?" The Queen yelled.

"They killed him, they killed him" He angrily repeated.

"They killed who?" Naomi asked.

"The White Man." He yelled as he slammed the door closed.

"Will you please just tell us what you're talking about." Naomi insisted.

"Dr. King, they killed him. They killed the man."

The joy in the room quickly turned silent as we all went into an instant state of shock.

"What?" I asked.

This was the first time in my fourteen years that The Queen was lost for words. Beatrice, Kathy and I quietly sat on the living room couch and began wiping tears from our watery eyes. I found myself unable to cope with the news so I stood up and headed for the stairs. Meanwhile, Douglass had made his way to the old television and turned it on to one of the local stations. As soon as the voice of the narrator was heard I knew this was the real thing.

"Dr. King was standing on the Balcony of the Loraine Hotel in Memphis, Tennessee when he was struck down by a single bullet." The news reporter said solemnly. At that point I slowly turned around and sat on the bottom step while attempting to wipe my eyes dry. Upset, Kathy quickly walked to the television and turned it off. Douglass, angry at her actions, quickly turned the television back on and sat on a nearby chair to prevent Kathy from turning the television off again. The room remained quiet for hours as the news reports continued. Then suddenly as Dr. King's "I had a dream" speech played the entire family huddled on the couch and began reciting the end of the speech with him.

"And if America is to be a great nation this must become true. So let freedom ring from the prodigious hilltops of New Hampshire. Let freedom ring from the mighty mountains of New York. Let freedom ring from the heightening Alleghenies of Pennsylvania!

Let freedom ring from the snowcapped Rockies of Colorado!

Let freedom ring from the curvaceous peaks of California!

But not only that; let freedom ring from Stone Mountain of Georgia!

Let freedom ring from Lookout Mountain of Tennessee!

Let freedom ring from every hill and every

molehill of Mississippi. From every mountainside, let freedom ring.

When we let freedom ring, when we let it ring from every village and every hamlet, from every state and every city, we will be able to speed up that day when all of God's children, black men and white men, Jews and Gentiles, Protestants and Catholics, will be able to join hands and sing in the words of the old Negro spiritual, "Free at last! Free at last! Thank God Almighty, we are free at last!"

As soon as the speech ended Mae began crying as if she knew the impact of Dr. King's death on the country.

Friday April 5, 1968

9:00 a.m.

That next day I arrived at school exhausted from staying up until the wee hours of the night. My body was limp and found it difficult to concentrate. To my surprise the other kids seem energetic and full of life.

"Did they just not hear the news?" I said to myself.

"That had to be the case", I convinced myself, "or otherwise they would feel like me." I continued thinking.

"Hey Kim." Bunny said as we approached our neighbouring lockers.

"Hi, so I guess you didn't hear the news." I asked.

"What news?"

"Dr. King, he was shot and killed last night."

"Oh, I know about that, so what." He said as our homeroom teacher Mrs. Nicholson walked by.

"Who got shot?" Tonya, another classmate asked approaching Bunny and I.

"Dr. King" I replied.

"Who?" Tonya asked.

"You know, Martin Luther King Jr." I said raising my voice.

"Who's he?" Tonya asked.

"Have you been living in some type of cave or something? He was trying to fight against this stupid country so that us blacks could have better jobs and housing and other stuff." I replied.

"Oh girl, I don't have time to worry about that stuff, I have other things to do." Tonya said as she raced behind a group of passing boys.

"Gosh, how can somebody be so dumb?" I thought shaking

my head.

"So what, he's dead, people die every day. What, you're gonna get upset every time somebody kicks the bucket." Bunny said.

"No, but Dr. King was different." I replied.

"Ah so what, the man made a few speeches, who cares." Bunny said.

Bunny's comments were heartless and unappreciated; Well, what did I expect from a guy who didn't shed one tear when his best friend was killed right in front of him. Disgusted at Bunny and his sour attitude I quickly slammed my locker closed, headed into my homeroom and sat at my old wooden desk near the front of the room. I was so angry at Bunny that I wanted to ring his neck, but instead I just cried. I didn't know whether my anger was because I was tired or because I was upset over Dr. King's death or because I was mad at Bunny or was it a combination of all three.

As I looked at the other students in my homeroom class, I was shocked at the party like atmosphere they displayed. When I left for school that morning, I thought the day would be full of sorrow and anger but that was not the case. There was laughter, playing and joking as if nothing had happened.

"Students let's come to order." Mrs. Nicholson commanded. The class quickly obeyed her command as Mrs. Nicholson was no joke and was a force to be reckoned with.

"Alright, I guess, you all have heard by now that Dr. King was assassinated last evening." She continued.

"Thank the Lord", I said to myself. I was so glad she said something because I was beginning to believe that I was the only one that cared.

"Today, we will not have our normal homeroom or first

period. We will quietly go down to the auditorium and watch a film on the civil rights movement and from some of the conversations I've heard this morning some of you need to see it." She finished.

"I don't see why we need to waste a whole morning looking at some stupid film." Bunny said.

"Bunny do you know anything about our history?" Mrs. Nicholson said.

"Yeah, I know enough."

"And what do you know." Mrs. Nicholson asked.

"I know that we came here on boats and we were slaves but now we're not." Bunny explained.

"Is that all you know." Mrs. Nicholson said as the bell rang.

"We'll talk when we get back. Now everyone line up at the door." Mrs. Nicholson said realizing that it was now time to head to the auditorium.

&

After returning to the classroom some two hours later Mrs. Nicholson kept her promise and had a long discussion with the class on the impact of the Civil Rights movement on black society. The lesson seem to have an effect on Bunny as he began to realize the impact of Dr. Kings' death on us blacks. But it had no effect on boy crazy Tonya. No matter what Mrs. Nicholson said nothing seem to get through to her, it was just hopeless. Her passive attitude left most of the class wondering if there was indeed a brain between her oversize ear loathes.

"Attention students and teachers." The Principle's voice rang over the intercom. "Because of student protest at Northwestern High School the administration has decided to implement emergency plan code red. As a result, students are to remain in their present classrooms until school is dismissed at 2:30 this afternoon. Students however will be allowed to go to the cafeteria during normal lunch hours, but each teacher is to accompany them to, from and during their lunch periods. Students needing to use the rest rooms must be escorted by security. There are no exceptions to these rules and anyone who breaks them will be removed from school premises. "The Principle concluded.

"What happened at Northwestern?" Bunny asked.

"I have no idea, but whatever it was must have been serious." Mrs. Nicholson said.

Later that day we found out that groups of students at Northwestern High School and Coppin State College refuse to follow normal procedures in response to Dr. King's death. My understanding was that there was no violence, just defiance, which led to several arrests. We were also told that each school was given the option of implementing their emergency plans, if desired, and my school elected to implement our school's emergency plan.

Saturday April 6, 1968

8:00 a.m.

Two days after the assassination of Dr. King the family began feeling the effects of sleep degradation as we spent the last two days watching the news into way pass midnight. Our biological clocks were now confusing night and day and were refusing to let us sleep during normal sleeping hours. Tired of working to fall asleep that chilly day Naomi and I decided to sit on the front steps of our brick house row house to watch the world go by. As Naomi watched me mindlessly pick dry grass pieces off the steps two geriatric neighbors from a few doors down approached us.

"Hi, Mr. Ray, Mr. Hammon" Naomi said.

"Hello Ladies." The two men said stopping in front of our steps.

"I guess you've heard about Dr. King?" Mr. Hammon asked.

"Yeah, we've been staying up the last two nights lookin' at the news." Naomi said.

"Same for my family." Mr. Hammon said.

"I just wonder how this country is goin' to survive without his persistence and hard work. He did so much for the country and for people of all races." He continued.

"We've been wondering that ourselves." Naomi said.

The four of us stared at each other in silence for the next five or so minutes when suddenly Douglass races out of the house dressed in his Black Panther Uniform.

"Move!" He said pushing me aside to make his way down the steps.

"I hate you, you idiot." I yelled.

"What?" He said looking at me in shock.

"You heard what I said." I responded.

"So, when did you become so mouthy?" Douglass asked confused.

"Since you people started getting on my nerves."

"Look little sis..."

"No, you look. I'm so tired of you and your Black Panther friends, your drug buddies and everybody else you hang with. You come in here Thursday night acting like you are so upset over Dr. King's death, yet you are a member of a group that stands for everything he didn't believe in. Just look at you, if Dr. King saw you lookin' stupid like that he would take you to a dark room and talk some sense into..."

"Hey look, don't down my friends. It's gonna' be people like H. Rap whose gonna make sure this sorry ass country don't put us back twenty years." Douglass yelled interrupting.

"I understand Brown is now organizing groups of protestors." Mr. Hammond said.

"Yeah man, we're gonna' show the white man that we mean business."

"Please!" I said disgusted.

Upset over my comments Douglass made his way down the cold steps and headed north toward North Ave.

"Hey I'm proud of you." Naomi said giving me a hug.

"Yeah, he really deserved that." Mr. Hammond said.

"Definitely." Mr. Ray said as a large group of people distracted him while they loudly walked toward us.

"Hey what's going on?" Mr. Ray said to the group.

"There's a rally at Lafayette Square in an hour." One male member of the group said.

"For what?" Naomi asked.

"CORE has sat up a rally at the Metropolitan Church. They want us poor people's opinion as how to best handle any problems that may occur because of Dr. King's death." The group member said.

"I don't get it. What do you mean?" I asked.

"CORE is afraid violence may break out." Another group member said.

"But why would that happen?" I responded.

"Hey, Negroes in this city are angry. The city of Baltimore has done very little to stop desegregation and with Dr. King's death it just might put fuel into those that are already on fire."

"Yeah, but the state seems to care about Dr. King's death. The news said that Governor Agnew ordered all Maryland flags to be flown at half-staff until after the funeral." Naomi said.

"Yeah this is the same guy who refused to listened to a group of Bowie State College students about the terrible conditions at the school." The member said.

"And anyway, who gives a damn about some dumb flags. Most of us want action." He continued.

"Yeah!!" The crowd screamed.

"So, you guys in?" The man asked.

"Yeah, sure." We all said without hesitation.

Naomi and I joined the crowd as it made its way toward Pennsylvania Avenue and then toward Lafayette Square. During the walk the crowd sang spiritual songs, told stories of discrimination and reminisced about Dr. King and others who fought to make life better for everybody. Before we knew it the energy of each person combined to form a union stronger and more intense then the sun. For some the energy level was so overwhelming that several older women fell to their knees.

It was like a scene out of a movie when several men surrounded the women in an attempt to comfort them. This site brought tears from every member of the crowd, forcing the formation of many small comforting groups. Eventually the desires of the crowd to participate in the Lafayette Square gathering gave us the strength to re-group and make it to our destination.

As we approached the large gathering of some two hundred people I stopped and soaked up the intense emotions resonating from the group of Negro men, women and children. The gathering was energetic to say the least. There were people from all over the West side, each with their own stories of racism and hatred. Most were screaming to the top of their lungs in an effort to drown out the sounds of other group members. It made for a distracting and confusing gathering, which made me wonder how was this group going to come together and make any decisions.

Though tempted to turn around and go home I decided to make my way to the front of the crowd where I had noticed a small child whose eyes were following my every move. The little girl could not have been any older than four years old. Her wavy brown hair was combed into four neat long ponytails, just right for a girl of her small stature. Her large brown eyes were mesmerizing and drew me into her world as if she was a Princess. When I got to arm's length of the young girl I instantly stopped, staring at her beautiful brown skin. She then drew the biggest smile on her tiny face and I smiled in return.

"Ok, quiet" I loud masculine voice was heard from an older

stocky gentleman facing the front of the crowd.

"I do not want to repeat myself but if I have to I will and then I will gracefully escort out any and all of you who cannot follow my directions." The man continued in a louder voice some minutes later.

The crowd then quickly follows orders and waits for the gentleman to give further direction.

"Thank you" The man said impatiently.

"I know the events of the last few days have left our community in a state of disarray and I project that some of us will be tempted to commit all kinds of violent acts in retaliation for the death of Dr. King. "

"You bet" A young man angrily yelled.

"I know that you believe that we should act all nice and goody-to-shoes like nothing ever happened but I won't do that. I'm so tired of walking around with blinders on." Another male voice said.

"We will not be walking around with blinders on. We will be demonstrating the professionalism and maturity of our people while still carrying on the work of Dr. King." The Stocky man continued.

"The hell with that. Look at where that got him." The second man yelled.

"Dr. King knew that his work would someday cost him his life but he didn't believe in violence to perform his job. If you believe that violence is the only way to resolve racial issues, then you are at the wrong rally." The Stocky man continued.

"Then maybe I am." The young man said.

"Then you are stupid." I blurted out without thought.

"You go ahead and joint one of those violent groups and you will see who comes out on top. And I bet, it will not be you. You will be digging your own grave and accomplishing nothing but causing the deaths of our people. You better think before you leave this rally." I continued.

The young man put his head down in shame as the rest of the crowd nodded their heads in agreement. Despite the anger expressed by the young man, the group, including the man, focused and was able to help the organizers get the information they needed to help alleviate any anticipated troubles. In my eyes the gathering was a success, to some others it was a waste of time as they believed violence was the only way we could get our point across to the city and the state.

Saturday April 6, 1968

11:015 p.m.

Later that evening the family had gathered at Uncle Marvin's house to celebrate the upcoming Easter Holiday. Despite the somber mood of the city our family gathering was quite enjoyable. There was food from every animal group, beef, pork, poultry and seafood. My uncle and grandmother also spoiled us with tons of Macaroni and Cheese, lots of Collar Greens, corn bread, corn and gallons upon gallons of soda pop. Man, my stomach was so stuffed; I felt like an old man when I had to loosen my pants just to sit on the couch.

"Hey Guys, be careful going home. I understand there's been looting in your area." Uncle Marvin said as he helped the Queen put on her coat before opening the front door.

"In our area?" The Queen asked.

"That's my understanding. I'm not sure but I heard rumors of problems on Pennsylvania Ave., several stores were broken into." He continued.

"You're kidding." The Queen responded.

"Do you know which stores were hit?" The Queen continued.

"I heard that The Inner City World Furniture Store was hit pretty hard."

"Good." I yelled.

"Kimberly!" Uncle Marvin said.

"I'm sorry Uncle Marvin, it's just that the owner treated us so badly when we went to buy a kitchen set a few weeks back." I explained.

"Yeah, a lot of folks can't stand that Mr. Shipiro." Naomi said.

"Yeah, he is a character." The Queen said.

"I don't get it; how does this guy stay in business with his nasty attitude." I said

"I don't' think that he's as bad as you think, I mean we keep buying from him." Naomi replied.

"Yes he is!" Beatrice said.

"He has all kinds of psychological issues. Frankly I believe he suffers from a Napoleon complex". Beatrice continued.

"Okayyyy, I guess we better go now." The Queen said after we all stood in silence for a few seconds trying to understand Beatrice's comment.

After picking up Mae from a nearby couch the Queen then walked slowly to Uncle Marvin, looks him lovingly in his large brown eyes and then gives him a tight hug.

"Thanks for the money, I really appreciated it." She said to him in a low voice

"I'm just glad you're okay now." Uncle Marvin said before kissing her on the left cheek.

The Queen, Naomi, Beatrice, Mae, Kevin and I then headed through the front door. From the second we walked out the door I was overcome with the most eerie feeling. There were no cars, no trucks, no people. The darkness of the night revealed illusions of ghostly figures floating through our bodies as we naively walked through the dimly lit streets. These figures seem to sit quietly in the sparse trees as the still atmosphere sent chills down my thin arms. Unaware of the reasons behind the desolated streets we continued our walk from Druid Park Lake Drive toward our home on Preston Street.

While cautiously approaching North Ave., in now complete darkness, we noticed several large green vehicles driving through the intersection of North Ave. and Smallwood Streets. Visually the site was distracting but the loud sounds of silence continued deafening our ears as the eerie feelings of the dark night had encompassed us all.

As we approached the intersection of Smallwood Street and North Avenue the large green vehicle presence dominated the existence of the common man, personal and public vehicles and even domestic animals. The security we all felt earlier that evening slowly dwindled with the passing of each vehicle as we weren't sure as to what was going on.

"Hey they look like Army men!!" Kevin yelled breaking the silence.

"I think you're right." The Queen said reluctantly.

"Kim, how come there are so many Army men?" Kevin asked.

"I don't know." I said as Kevin ran ahead.

"Kevin!!" We all screamed as he ran to the intersection.

"Come back here." The Queen yelled as Kevin turned the corner to North Ave.

A split second after Kevin turned the corner a loud noise was heard forcing us to run faster to catch up with him. After turning the corner, a site we never imagined was placed before us as Kevin lay quietly on the cold sidewalk with a large hole in the left side of his chest. His normally energetic body was now as limp as a dead snake while blood poured aggressively from the gaping hole.

"Kevin, my God, you shot him, you ass-holes." The Queen yelled as she noticed several National Guards men running toward Kevin.

"Ma'am, there was a 10:00 curfew put into effect." A white Baltimore City Policeman said approaching the group.

"I'm sorry about your boy, but he should not have been on the streets." He said nonchalantly walking toward us.

"Did you shoot him?" I violently screamed.

"Yeah, but he should not have been on the streets." The Police officer continued.

"So now what, you're going to shoot us all?" The Queen said wiping blood from Kevin's chest.

"I should Niggers, instead I'll just send your asses to jail for breaking curfew." He said as other Police officers gathered around Kevin's body.

"Arrest them and call for an ambulance." He ordered of the others as we tended to Kevin.

"I hate you, I hate you, I hate you." I yelled. "If he dies, I'll find you and kill you." I finished before being dragged off.

"Hey where are you taking her?" The Queen yelled.

"Th same place you're goin'" A Police Officer replied.

"And where the hell is that?" She continued as the other officers began dragging the rest of the group toward an awaiting Patrol car.

"Jail." He replied.

"Hell no, I'm staying with my baby." The Queen said attempting to pull away from her arresting officer. Suddenly the Police officer tending to Kevin pulls out a gun and points it at The Queen.

"Nigger, if you take one more step I'll kill you." He angrily said.

"Mother please, just come with us, please." Naomi begged.

After a long pause the Queen decides to walk quietly to the awaiting car, where Beatrice and I had already been placed in the back seat. As the police carelessly stuffed Naomi and the

Queen in the back seat, I noticed the officer pressing hard on Kevin's tiny chest. With each press his body arched and his head went back. Blood seem to flow faster and faster from the hole in his chest with each press of the officer's hands. As the car drove off one of the officers began putting a blanket over Kevin's still body.

"Good bye my brother, good-bye." I said to myself as I performed our special good-bye hand game.

"I love you." I finished while crying.

&

As we pulled up to the same Police station, I visited just weeks earlier, I noticed the calm of that evening was not to be found. There was a constant movement of people, mostly Negroes escorted by white Police officers. The facial expressions of the escorted men, women and yes children, showed signs of beaten wear. As we exited the car the cries of screaming children rang loudly through the air as their mothers attempted to comfort them.

While we were being escorted by our white attendants toward the large crowd, I recognized the same little girl from the rally. I made eye contact with the little girl. Her large, now blood shot eyes, told me the story of her long night as dried tears filled her eye sockets and lined her cheeks. Sensing her desire to abandon the situation I nodded my head to let her know that everything would be okay. Her eyes then widen as if to say thank you. Continuing to stare and smile at me for a couple of seconds she then slowly turned to head for the ever-growing crowd with her over-weight adult female companion.

Some two hours were spent waiting outside before entering the station. By that time the crowd had doubled making for an uncontrollable situation. Several groups of young Negro teens attempted to break from the crowd triggering the militia style Police Officers to physically attack, hand cuff and drag them bleeding and hurt into the station.

As we finally entered the old Police building, we were greeted by an equal number of people as was outside. For the most part it was standing room only but some had found little areas on the cold concrete floor to sit. The tone of the room was somber and the faces of the awaiting crowd were worn. Periodically, officers would appear from several tall metal doors to escort a handful of Negroes to the mysterious rooms in the back.

Two hours passed when we were finally called to one of those rooms. Entering the small room we noticed a white man wearing a black robe sitting behind a small brown wooden table.

"Come in." The man said before we filled the tiny room.

"I'm Judge Harris. (Pause) So you folks were caught breaking curfew on North Ave." He continued.

"But we didn't know there was a curfew." The Queen said.

"That's no excuse." The Judge said.

"It is when you're the one arrested for something you didn't know was a crime." The Queen argued.

"Miss. Carter don't argue with me."

"Why not, I'm tired, my six-year-old is laying shot on North Avenue and I'm pissed at the treatment we have received since we got here."

"Miss. Carter I can have you thrown in jail for the next week if you don't shut up."

"Mother, please, I want to go home." Beatrice whined.

"Yes mother, please. We are all tired." Naomi said.

As usual the Queen gave into Naomi's request and stopped talking. After looking angrily at the judge, she retreated quietly to the left corner of the room.

"You handle things." She said to Naomi.

"I'm sorry sir. My family was not aware of the curfew; I promise we will not break the curfew again." Naomi said to the judge.

"Okay young lady. I believe you. You are all released. But make sure you keep your mother's mouth shut." The judge said.

"I will." Naomi said before we left the room and walked through the large crowd toward the door.

"Hey you folks aren't leavin', are you?" A middle-aged Negro man said.

"Yeah, we've been here long enough." The Queen replied.

"No, you have to stay here until 6:00 am." He said.

"Why, that's two hours away. I hate this place. It's crowded, it's dark, it smells like pee and I damn tired of seeing these stupid ass racist police." The Queen said.

"Hey look lady, I was brought in here at 11:00 and released at 12:45. When I left at 1:00 and headed home I was re-arrested and now I'm back. I tried to explain to those stupid police officers that I was just here but they could care less.", The man continued.

"What?" The Queen said in disbelief.

"Yeah, you're better off waiting here for the two hours." The man said.

Disappointed, we found several small spots next to a wall and sat on the cold floor until 6:00 am. As soon as we received confirmation that the curfew had been lifted for the day, we made our way to a nearby bus stop. Hungry, dirty and exhausted our small group waited patiently for the number twenty-eight bus to Randallstown, which makes a stop at Provident Hospital some four miles north of the police station. Our group said not one word as we waited the thirty-five minutes for a bus. Finally, one arrived and we boarded one by one to take seats in the rear.

Passing city street scenes in the small bus window reminded me of news footage of Vietnam. The National Guard presence was shown throughout each business district along the route. As we passed Mondawmin Mall the National Guard, Baltimore City Police and other law enforcement officers caring guns and other assault weapons, surrounded the premises. Negroes passing through the area were stopped and seem to be harassed.

The scenes from outside had every passenger on the bus immersed in curiosity, that was until the smell of reefer immerged from the rear of the bus. The Queen, though tired and worn, got up, walked to the back where several teenage boys were the source of the smell, stood angrily above them not saying one word. Scared for their lives they put the reefer cigarettes out and stared ahead in fear. The Queen then retreated to her seat with the family and continued looking at the scenes from the bus's small passenger window.

Sunday April 7, 1968

8:10 am

At the time, we had no idea if Kevin had been taken to Provident Hospital or if he was lying dead in some morgue somewhere. The National Guard was heartless to our need to accompany him while he laid lifeless on the cold ground; they wouldn't even let the Queen stay with him. There were times, during that six hours, I thought Kevin was dead and that's why they didn't want any of us to stay. But I had to stop myself from thinking that way and had to believe that he was okay.

When we finally arrived at Provident hospital a large group of angry people were attempting to make their way through the front doors of the building. The crowd was so large that the Bus Driver had to let us off more than a thousand feet from the bus stop.

"What is all this?" Naomi said.

"I don't know." The Queen replied as we made our way toward the crowd.

"Hey can somebody tell me what's goin' on?" The Queen yelled.

"They won't let us in." A woman said.

"Why not?" The Queen asked.

"Because they don't want you Niggers crowding up their precious hospital." An angry man said.

"With all the looting and fires lots of people were hurt and were brought here. Now everybody on the West side is here to check on their love ones.

Apparently, there've been too many for the hospital to handle. So not only are they turning away victims they're not letting any family members in either." The woman finished.

"But my six-year-old was shot last night, I need to get to him." The Queen replied.

"You and every other mother." The angry man said.

The crowd of about seventy people tried repeatedly to get the attention of hospital personnel by banging uncontrollably on the glass entrance doors each time someone walked by. The crowd's patience was wearing thin as the minutes ticked and the hospital workers continued to ignore us.

"Hey, open this damn door." The angry man said as a nurse walked by the large glass doors.

True to form she behaved as others before her, in that her nonchalant arrogant attitude had her ignoring the crowd and going about her business. This drove the crowd to the point where several people picked up baseball sized rocks and began throwing them at the glass doors. Within several minutes a small crack appeared and within fifteen more minutes a hole the size of a basketball was visible.

Suddenly, several Baltimore City Police cars raced to the hospital parking lot to make their way to the crowd. After the cars came to complete stops the Police, armed with drawn guns, ran toward the now outraged crowd.

"Everybody, move away from the doors" One Police man said.

"Hey my daughter's in this damn place and I wanna' see her." The angry man said.

"What did I say you Niggers." The same Police man said approaching the man.

The crowd, including the man, anticipating Police action slowly moved away from the doors and stood by a nearby lamp post. But to everyone's surprise no actions were taken.

After one of the Officers approached the door it opened and several Nurses carrying clip boards walked out.

"Thank you Officers." Said a white middle age nurse.

"Folks I'm sorry about this situation. We have been inundated with victims and families since the riots started. We want you to know that we are here to serve you. So, what we're going to do is have everyone line up and I will talk to each of you in turn. I have a list of people who have been admitted, a list of people who were brought here but have been discharged or have died. (Slight Pause) If your loved one is still here you will be escorted by security to the appropriate areas, otherwise please leave the premises quickly. Is everyone clear on the procedures?" She concluded.

"Yeah!" The crowd yelled as they quickly formed a line.

My mother, Naomi and I took spots at the end of the line as we realized we were the last to arrive. But our last place status didn't last very long as several groups of arriving people peacefully took their places behind us.

"Please let Kevin be in there, please." I repeated to my self during the one and a half hours my family and I stood in line.

"Yes Ma'am, who are you looking for?" The Nurse politely said to The Queen as we approached her.

"We're looking for Kevin Carter." The Queen said.

"No, no Kevin Carter here." She stated after going down the list.

My heart instantly dropped into my stomach at the unexpected comment. Waiting for the nurse to confirm that Kevin had been taken to the morgue slowly drained the life from me as if drawn out by a powerful magnet.

"Nurse, he is a little boy, six-years old. He was shot last night." Naomi said as the nurse continued looking over the list.

"Okay, we do have a John Doe that fits that description. Guard, show them inside. They need to go to ICU-8." The Nurse said after re-reading her list.

The white Guard calmly escorted us to a desk where several nurses were waiting.

"Yes." One of them said.

"These ladies need to go to ICU-8." The Guard said.

"Okay, you ladies come with me." A Nurse instructed.

"Good luck ladies, I hope everything turns out okay with your loved one." The Guard said as we proceeded to follow the Nurse.

"Thank you very much. "The Queen said.

"I'm sure he'll be fine." The Queen continued.

We were then escorted through several large groups of waiting people, all of whom who looked as if fatigue had sat in and death was just around the corner. There were little people, big people, medium size people but most of all they were all Negroes who have been caught up in an unintentional nightmare like us. That nightmare we shared seemed to be getting worse by the minute. Though I realized my family wasn't the only one in this turmoil I still felt as though we were isolated from the rest.

To me, they were not us and they had no idea what we were going through. They were just a bunch of poor people who would disappear as soon as I left that horrid building. They were just temporary images there to fill a frame in time. I didn't want to see those people; I couldn't wait to get away from them. I didn't feel sorry for any of them. My main concern was my youngest brother so I could care less about what they were going through. After arriving at the elevators,

I attempted to bond with those people by staring each of them in their eyes, but my body iced and my eyes blinded.

As the elevator operator opened the doors the accompanying nurse instructed her to take us to the eighth floor. The operator nodded as we entered then closed the doors. Except for the playing music the elevator remained quiet as it slowly made its way to the eighth floor. Once stopped, the elevator doors opened and my nervous group fixated on the sterile white walls.

Noticing our hesitation, the accompanying nurse slowly stepped off the elevator, turned around and looked compassionately in our eyes, waiting patiently for us to join her. With a cue from the Queen the four of us disembarked and followed the Nurse through several long and cold hallways. Signs of sorrow filled every inch of the long hallway where several patient rooms reside. The smell of formaldehyde overwhelmed our senses keeping the thought of death in our minds.

The medium sized white nurse finally approached the desk where another nurse was sitting. After a brief conversation, the two nurses approached our frightened group.

"Good morning." The Second Nurse quietly said.

"Good morning." We all replied in low voices.

"The young boy in this room is about four feet tall, weighs about fifty-five pounds and has a large birth mark on his..."

"Left side." My mother said interrupting.

"Yes." The Nurse replied.

"That sounds like Kevin." I said loudly.

"Well, okay, seems like our little John Doe has a family." The Second nurse replied happily.

"I normally only let the parents in, but since you folks have been through so much I'll let you all in." The Nurse explained after a short pause.

She then carefully opens the door, exposing Kevin laying in a bed two times his size. There were tubes coming out of everywhere, his mouth, his nose, just everywhere. Instantly my eyes watered and my hands shivered. The Queen, noticing my fear, puts her right arm around my shoulders and escorted me into the room.

"He's going to be okay." She said as we stopped at the foot of the bed.

The Queen then takes that right arm from around my shoulders then uses her right hand to wipe my ragged bangs from over my blood shot eyes.

"Okay Mommy." I said trying to hold back the tears.

"He's had a really difficult night." The Nurse said.

"He's had two surgeries, both of which went well. Now it's just a waiting game." She continued.

The four of us stayed by Kevin's side throughout the day, waiting for some signs of life. As the clock approached 2:00 p.m. our many prayers had gone unanswered. Kevin had yet to regain consciousness. His large brown eyes hadn't batted a single blink and his small hands were in the same position as they were at 10:00 a.m. that morning.

"Hello" A white man said entering, along with a black man.

"Hi." We all said trying to figure out who these men were.

"I'm Dr. Keith, I spent most of the night working on Kevin. Of course, at the time I didn't know his name." The white man said.

"Hi, I'm Dr. Holmes." The black man said.

"I'm the surgeon that operated on this fine young man." He continued.

When the black man introduced himself as a surgeon my eyes almost popped out of my head. This was the first time I had ever seen a Negro doctor. Hey, I didn't know that Negro men did much more than run stores, collect garbage, drive buses, join gangs and fight for civil rights.

"Hi I'm Miss. Carter Kevin's mother." The Queen said introducing herself to the calm doctors.

"Miss. Carter." Dr. Holmes said.

"Yes Doctor." My mother replied.

"Your son was shot on the left side of his chest. Let me show you." Dr. Holmes said.

He then walked to Kevin, removed the sheets from his upper torso and exposed his entire bandaged left chest.

"The bullet entered three inches to the left of his heart, approximately right here." He continued as he pointed to a small area of Kevin's left chest.

"Now, as the bullet entered his tiny body it hit a rib, did some damage to this left lung then existed through his back. Because of this I repaired his lung, closed both the entry and exit points and wrapped his chest so his rib will heel normally." He concluded.

"Will he be okay?" I asked crying.

"Yes, young lady. I believe so. He's young and in excellent condition." He answered.

"But he just lays there." I said crying.

"That's because we have him sedated for right now."

"How long do you think he will be in the hospital?" My mother asked.

"That's hard to say. It depends on how well he does after we wake him up." Dr. Holmes replied.

"Dr. Holmes and I are confident that Kevin will have very little, if any, long term effects from this unfortunate incident." Dr. Keith explained while looking at his watch.

"Ladies, I have an appointment on another floor so I will leave you with Dr. Holmes and I will check on Kevin later." Dr. Keith said before leaving the room.

"Miss Carter, young ladies are there any questions or concerns." Dr. Holmes asked.

"No, I just have to figure out how to pay for all this." My mother said thinking out loud.

"Oh, that's been taken care of." Dr. Holmes explained.

"I'm not sure, but the National Guard representative who stayed with him through the night said everything was taken care of." Dr. Holmes continued.

"You know, God was listening." My mother said after a long pause.

"I've been praying since last night that first my son would survive and second that we won't lose our home because we have to pay medical bills. Thank you, Lord." She continued.

Monday April 8, 1968

5:03 am

It had been four days since Dr. King's assassination and Baltimore City was still in a state of turmoil. Riots had broken out on both sides of the city, looters had destroyed many businesses in predominately Negro areas, thousands of people had been arrested for curfew violations and hundreds of people had been hurt or killed. It was now Monday and instead of spending the day in school the city had ordered all schools close until further notice. The city had also instated gasoline rations as well as a band on alcohol sales.

My neighborhood, Druid Heights, was especially hit hard by the riots as we lost many of the businesses that served the area. Pennsylvania Ave., where Mr. Parkinston's store was located looked like a war zone. National Guards men stood cautiously along the streets in an attempt to deter the violence and looting. As we returned from the hospital that previous night, we were forced to take a less than direct route home due to the horrific activities on Pennsylvania Ave. and its surrounding streets.

We learned later that to our surprise Mr. Parkinston, the Greek store, and Laura's Furniture store remained intact. That was more than I could say for most of the other businesses in the Pennsylvania Ave. corridor. Most had been totally destroyed either by fire or by the hands of Robin Hood thieves.

Many of our neighbors stayed indoors that week before Easter in fear of the many shootings across the city. But despite the unrest, my family ventured out each day to visit Kevin and today was no exception. Things were more organized at the hospital that Monday, that is compared to previous days. At least that day we only stood in line for an hour instead of the one and a half hours we stood in line the day before.

Kevin's condition remained the same as that first day. But because of our talk with the Doctors I was not worried.

It was now 11:00 p.m., one hour after curfew, and the entire family except Douglass was home and accounted for. Douglass' presence had been non-existence since early Saturday morning. He may have been missed by other members of the family, but I could care less and was hoping that he would never come back. Douglass' lack of compassion for the one sister who gave him every chance in the world, who believed that he could turn his life around; just how could he put me in a position that cost me my most precious gift.

The more I thought of that day the stronger my anger grew. At the time, I just knew I would celebrate if the cops banged on the door and told us that Douglass had been taken away to some far-off place or even killed.

During dinner, there was very little conversation and very little eye contact. Hand signals were used to jest for someone to pass plates of food. The Queen, usually full of sarcastic comments, could only part her lips to stuff food between them.

"Oh, I need a cup of coffee." The Queen said after shaking her head.

"Yes Ma'am." I said as I began to stand up and make the coffee.

"No, you finish your meal, you do enough around here." She said putting her hand on my left shoulder as she walked toward the stove.

Her positive comment sent chills up my spine as this was

the first time she ever she acknowledged the work I did around the house. This sudden burst of appreciation brought a small smile on my face. Then Suddenly a loud knock was heard at the door.

"Who could that be?" Kathy asked.

"I have no idea." My mother said walking towards the door.

I couldn't help think about my negative thoughts about Douglass as my mother walked toward the door. I really didn't mean those things I thought earlier; I didn't want anything bad to happen to him. As my mother approached the door my heart began beating so hard that I was waiting for it to burst into a million pieces. The stress became unbearable, but quickly changed to a sigh of relief when Mrs. Wilson walked in.

"Good afternoon, my favorite neighbors." Mrs. Wilson Happily said.

"Annie, don't you know there's a curfew in effect." My mother said.

"Look, it's bad enough this stupid city wants me to hang a black sock on my house to show that I'm black. Now if the city of Baltimore has an issue with me visiting my next-door neighbors then that's their problem.

"Annie, you will never change."

"So how's my little man doin'?"

"The same, but we have hope." My mother responded.

"Oh Kevin's a stubborn little boy, he won't let a stupid bullet take him out of this world." Mrs. Wilson said.

"Yeah, I guess that stubbornness comes from me." The Queen replied.

"You know Delores I must agree with that statement."

"Oh hush Annie." My mother said as the two of them walked into the kitchen.

"Hi Mrs. Wilson." I said.

"Hello Kimberly, how are you doing?" Mrs. Wilson asked while rubbing my back.

"Okay, I guess." I replied.

"Now don't you worry about Kevin. Naomi and I have spoken with God and he assures us that he will be okay." Mrs. Wilson said.

"Yes Ma'am." I responded.

"So what's goin' on outside." My mother asked.

"The same. I swear yesterday I thought there was no more stuff to be looted and burned but these people still manage to find something'." Mrs. Wilson stated.

"Is the National Guard still out there?" Beatrice asked.

"Yeah, what good that's doin'. You know I've lived in this area for over fifty years and it just disturbs me how much it's changed, and not for the better. I remember growing up the Royal Theatre was the hottest place around. It brought some of the hottest black singers and musicians to the area. The place was a hot spot of fine Negro culture. Oh it was great, every Friday and Saturday night Pennsylvania Ave. was hopping with classic musicians like Pearl Baily, Ethel Waters and Louie Armstrong. Man, those were fun times. You know, when they turned The Royal Theatre into a movie theatre the neighborhood starting going downhill. It went from a place to live to what some now call a ghetto." Mrs. Wilson explained.

"Now the place to live is Randallstown." Beatrice said.

"Exactly and I have no idea why, have you been out there?" Mrs. Wilson replied.

"No" Beatrice said.

"Randallstown is just a bunch of houses I heard." Beatrice continued.

"I know, there's no Negro culture out there, it's just a bunch of us out there who rarely talk to each other and whose heads are so high up in the air they've lost their since of culture." Mrs. Wilson said.

"Yeah, Negroes think because they move out of the ghetto they are no longer Negroes." My mother said.

"Well enough of my complaining, you know I could go on all day about our people. I came over to tell you that Douglass called and he said he was safe." Mrs. Wilson explained.

"Where is he?" My mother asked.

"He wouldn't tell me."

"Oh, I hope that boy lives to his next birthday. He's just gotten himself into all kinds of criminal things. I wish he could be more like Naomi, Beatrice and Kimberly." The Queen said.

"Hey I'm tryin'." Kathy said.

"But you're not trying hard enough." Mrs. Wilson said.

During the next couple of hours Mrs. Wilson and The Queen lectured Kathy on her free life, tellin' her that it was on a down ward spiral and doesn't seem to be gettin' any better. Of course, Kathy agreed with everything they said but her body language said something different. At that point I wondered if she would ever change.

Chapter 13

Returning To Normal

Dr. King's funeral was held on Tuesday April 9, 1968. It was televised by several stations and was watched by thousands across the country. His funeral seemed to signal the beginning of the end of the riots, violence and looting of the streets of Baltimore. When all was said and done over fifty-five-hundred people had been arrested and charged with curfew violations, over five-hundred teens, mostly black young males were arrested for a multitude of crimes and many were killed or injured.

By the end of the week most of the rioting and violence had subsided but never the less Governor Agnew continued to impose restrictions on gun sales until April fifteenth.

On April 16 Douglass returned from his MIA mission. He claimed he was staying with a friend in the county in order to avoid the violence in our area, like I believed that. Despite all that had happened since the day I lost my precious gift and with Kevin laying still in the hospital my hatred for Douglass continued to grow. Just to look at him made me sick to my stomach.

At least one thing, I noticed the Black Panther Uniform he was so proud of seem to have done a vanishing act. It's not that we hated the Black Panthers we were concerned more about Douglass' criminal actions. This time he had actually started wearing normal people clothes. Where he got the money for his new wardrobe, I had no clue. His new digs weren't flashy or anything and they actually made him look like a well-respected black man.

Along with the new wardrobe, Douglass' attitude also changed, and for the better. For some strange reason, he began helping out with Mae, escorting my mother back and forth to work, cleaning the house and looking for a job. His concern for Kevin surprisingly grew stronger as each day passed.

When not looking for a job or helping around the house he was sitting with Kevin, reading him stories, stroking his hair and whispering words of encouragement. After learning Kevin had developed an infection and that things didn't look too good Douglass spent every waking minute praying and watching over him.

But despite his sudden acts of compassion and his numerous attempts to get in my good graces I avoided him like the plague. Determined to redeem himself he actually had the nerve to follow me to the hospital one day. At first, I didn't realize he was behind me but when I turned the corner to head up war torn Pennsylvania Ave. he ran up and tapped me on my back.

"Hey little sis." He said with a puppy dog look.

"What?" I replied angrily.

"Are you goin' to the hospital?"

"So what if I am."

"I just wanna' walk with you. I mean it is a long walk for a young girl."

"So what, I've done it before." I angrily said walking away from him.

Douglass quickly runs up and continues to walk beside me despite my obvious anger.

"Go away, go away." I screamed as I stopped and turned to face him.

"But I just wanna' walk with you. He's my brother too." Douglass replied.

The more he groveled the more my anger intensified and the hotter my blood boiled.

"I wish you to the cornfield, I wish you to the cornfield." I said after tightly closing my eyes and putting both index fingers to either side of my temples.

"Damn." I said after opening my eyes and lowering my hands.

"You're still here."

"Look, I just want to apologize." He said as I continued to walk.

"Kim, please. I feel terrible about that day. I know I don't have a good excuse and I can't take back what happened, I just want to be your big brother again."

His comments were somewhat moving but my anger was stronger than ever. Giving into his begging would mean I was a sucker and gullible so I continued to walk toward the hospital. But Douglass was determined and would not let up.

&

The hospital smells and sounds begun to take a toll on me

after four hours of staring at a boy who hadn't moved in days. The repetitive calls for doctors who never seem to answer became the lyrics of a broken record forcing me to cover my ears each time it played. The Chinese water torture feeling admitted from a beeping machine had me ready to confess my utmost secrets and the sounds of Douglass' voice each time he spoke inspired me to open a nearby window and throw him out. But the sound most annoying was the silence of Kevin. He spoke not one word, he moved not one hand and he coughed not one cough.

From the moment I entered the room at 10:00 a.m. I worried that Kevin wouldn't pull through. Though Douglass was in the room there was no one to talk to, no one to express my feelings to. By 2:00 p.m. my thoughts of Kevin, the test, my dysfunctional family, Dr. King's death, and the suppression of Negroes had me wondering if Dr. King wasn't in a better place.

"This world stinks" I said to myself over and over again while watching Kevin.

"I hate this world." I thought.

Just thinking about everything that's happen had me realize that I wanted a better life than the one I was dealt, that I wanted to succeed but I knew it wasn't possible. Recent events had me realizing that the world was totally against Negroes.

"Maybe Douglass and Kathy have the right idea, maybe I shouldn't be so hard on them, maybe I should just join them or maybe I should just give up and join Dr. King." I thought to myself as I stared out of the window.

"Good afternoon, Kimberly." A nurse said breaking my trance and bringing me back to the real world.

"Good afternoon Nurse Williams." I said turning around

and wiping a few tears from my eyes.

"How's my little fellow doing today?" she asked.

"He still doesn't talk or move." I said.

"Yeah, is my brother going to live?" Douglass asked.

"Well Douglass, I know this looks pretty bad, but your brother is actually doing pretty well. All his vitals are normal. He does have a slight fracture but it seems to be healing."

"So why doesn't he wake up?" Douglass asked.

"Because he's been given drugs to keep him asleep."

"Yeah Douglass, you know what drugs can do to a person, right." I angrily said.

Douglass gave me the saddest puppy dog look I had ever seen on man or beast. After a quick look in my direction his eyes lowered to face the floor tearing as they redirected. Several long seconds passed before he shook his head and raised his eyes to refocus on me.

"Unfortunately, I do." He said wiping a tear or two.

"Well I guess we all have skeleton's in our closet." Nurse Williams said sensing the tension.

"Some more than others." I said.

I guess Douglass was not use to me back latching him because for the second time in a matter of days he got up and left.

"Don't be too hard on him." Nurse Williams said.

"Why not. Because of him and his stupid drugs I lost my virginity to a nose bleedin' ugly drug attic."

"What happened?"

After taking several minutes to, for the first time, tell somebody about the incident it seems like two thousand pounds were lifted off my thin shoulders. It felt good to talk about it to someone who didn't judge me and was far removed from the situation.

"Did you talk to your mother?"

"No I was afraid she would blame me."

"You'll be surprised."

"I don't know, she always blames me for everything."

"Well, sometimes mothers are hard on their children because they want them to live better lives than they did. Negro woman especially have struggled so much to get practically nowhere."

"What do you mean, you have a good job."

"Yeah, but us Negro Nurses will never make as much money as the white ones." She said.

"It's up to you young ones to progress forward. It's pretty much too late for us, especially since they killed Dr. King."

"Oh."

"Look, don't feel like what happened to you was your fault because you trusted your brother and he let you down. But also, remember that was in the past. You are okay, you did not become pregnant and you mentally grew. (Pause) I really think your brother feels bad about the incident."

"But I can't get that day out of my mind."

"I know and you never will. But please don't let it affect your future relationship with your brother and don't let it hurt your chances of succeeding in the future. Lord knows us Negro women have enough odds against us."

"I'll try." I said with no confidence.

"No, you will. But for right now why don't you catch up with Douglass to see how he's doing; Kevin is in good hands."

Despite that I let her advice go in one ear and out the other

I left Kevin and started my search for Douglass. The search didn't take long because as soon as I walked out the front doors of the hospital, I noticed him sitting on the curb. He was sitting next to two middle aged heavy set Negro men who appeared to be waiting for a bus.

"Hey, have you seen Harry lately." The first man said.

"No man, I haven't seen him in months." The second man said.

"Me neither." The first man responded.

"I think he stays in the house." The second man said.

"Yeah, I think he stays in the house too. What's up with that?" The first man asked.

"He ain't got no money." The second man answered.

"You think so man?" The first man asked.

"Yeah, he's poor, he's poorer than poor, he's so poor he don't even leave his house, he's so poor his cat ran away with some homeless guy in search of a better life." The second man responded.

"You know man I think you're right. Last time I saw that Negro he was checking his shoes for lost pennies." The first man said.

"Damn, my man got it bad." The second man said before a brief pause.

"You know, my man could be layin' in that house dead from starvation and we're sittin' here on his case." The first man said.

"Oh well, shoulda took that trash man job."

"Uh ha."

The two men said to each other as I walked pass and slowly sat next to Douglass. Noticing my presence and the conversation around us Douglass chuckled.

"You ready to go home." He said in a low voice.

"Yeah" I replied.

Chapter 14

Shocking Moments

Later that week I found myself alone in the dark dingy kitchen of our Preston Street row home. This did not bother me as I was tired of the rest of the world. At that point I could care less if any of the other residents of my home ever showed up again. I liked having the house to myself that way I could think about how to end my miserable existence on this God for saken' planet without interruption.

As I sat in front of the old nineteen inch black and white television, whose picture now resembled a winter wonderland, I contemplated the different ways to accomplish my task.

"Let's see, I could jump off a bridge or run out in front of a bus or maybe get Douglass's gun. (Pause) Nan, I can't do any of those they might hurt. Let's see, there's always sleeping pills. No can't do that either, I have a mental thing about taking more than one pill at a time and with my luck I'll fall asleep before I take enough to finish off the job. Well, there's always using a knife, but what if I survive then I'll be stuck with this big old scare on my wrist for the rest of my life. Damn, there's got to be a way. "I said laying on the couch contemplating and rejecting ever method of ending my life when suddenly a loud knock was heard from the front door.

"Kim, Kim please open the door, please!" A loud desperate voice screamed out.

Panicking, yet eager to see what was going on I ran and opened the door to discover Darlene sweating and in a daze.

"What's wrong?" I said after opening the door.

"Kim, Kim you've got to help me. Please help me." Darlene yelled ignoring my question and running into the house exasperated.

"What's wrong?"

"They're after me"

"Who's after you?"

"Douglass' gang."

Stunned at her response I quickly closed the door and cut the lights and t.v. off. Scared for our lives I quickly forced Darlene down the steps and into a basement closet where we turned on a dim light, closed the door behind us and sat in a far corner. As the two of us sat quietly I could see the tears pouring from my friend's eyes. I couldn't understand how a girl with such a perfect family could have possibly fallen into the claws of such of a violent group.

"I'm so sorry", she said.

"Why are you sorry?" I said.

"It's my fault the bleeder raped you."

"No it's not it's Douglass' fault."

"It's not, it's my fault. To get those idiots off my back I told the bleeder that you wanted to do it."

"What?"

"They caught me stealing drugs from them."

"I don't get it, how did you get mixed up with them?" I curiously asked.

Silence range in the small closet for a few minutes then all of a sudden Darlene burst into tears as a loud noise is heard from outside.

"Oh my God, oh my God" She screamed terrified.

"What's the matter?"

"They know where I am, they're coming to get me. Help me, help me, they're going to kill me"

"Darlene, what's wrong with you, clam down." I said interrupting.

"No, they're out to get me, I just heard them shooting." She said.

"That wasn't shooting it was a car back firing."

"Yes it was!" Darlene said paranoid.

"They have people everywhere. They're watching my every step. I saw them, I saw them, they all had guns. I saw them coming after me. (Pause) They were on the corners, they were trying to break into my house, so I ran out and I came here. (Pause) Oh my God, what's that?" She said panicking.

"What's what?" I asked.

"That!" She screamed pointing to the door.

"It's the door", I calmly said.

"No, there's something' comin' through the big hole in the middle of the door. Oh no, it's him, its him" She said even more panicky.

"Darlene, are you high, what's wrong with you? There's no hole in the door" I said confused.

"You're lyin', why are you lying to me. I thought you were my friend." Darlene said staring at the door.

Certain that my friend was high on some type of drug I watched as her eyes rowed back and forth, up and down while her hands sweat and her body shivered. After looking around the small room in a daze Darlene quickly runs to the door and begins banging out of control. Trying to prevent her from hurting her fragile hands I grabbed her right arm and attempted to pull her towards the back of the room.

"No, get away from me. Don't kill me, please don't kill me." She pleaded to the door.

"Nobody's goin' to hurt you, I promise, I promise." I said as she slowly began calming down and began to catch her breath.

"I'll tell you what, let's go next store to Mrs. Wilson's house. She'll protect you." I said as Darlene went from hysteria to just a sheer panic.

"Okay, okay, okay", she said calming down and looking around the small room.

After I carefully exited the small room and lead Darlene up the steps to the front door, I sang her favorite song to help keep her calm. Mid-way up the rickety stairs she began singing along with me. At that point her crisis seemed over. But as soon as I opened the front door, to my surprise, Darlene instantly returned to panic mode.

"They're everywhere Kim. Just look at them, they're coming at me. I know it and they all have knives and guns. I have to do something; I just have to do something." She said running to the kitchen and grabbing a knife.

"I'll get them" She chanted over and over again as she headed toward the front door waving the knife.

"Darlene, don't take that knife you might hurt somebody." I said trying to take the knife out of her hands.

"Leave me alone!" She said pointing the knife at me.

Despite all the thoughts of ending my own life I was scared at the possibility of my best friend ending it for me. It was at that moment I realized I had too much to live for. I had a long life ahead of me and I wanted to see it. At that point I was not going to let her end my life. In an attempt to ward off this stranger I backed away from the front door and just watched as this hundred-pound fourteen-year-old girl turned into a three-hundred-pound raving maniac.

To my relief, this drug created monster headed out the door, but then runs into the busy street where she was instantly hit by a passing truck.

&

Dear Diary,

I'm so sorry for the tone of our last conversation. I'm sorry to let you see how weak I had become from the everyday troubles of life in the ghetto. I will never let you see me like that again. I will never let these down falls bring me to a level I am not accustomed.

Today Diary, I saw my good friend paralyzed when she ran in front of a truck. Diary she was high on some type of drug. She's only 14 and now because of the choices she made she will spend the rest of her life in a wheelchair. Diary, I don't get it, she had everything. She has two parents that love her, she's doing great in school, and she had the support of her entire family. I just don't understand it. You know Diary, even though I feel sorry for Darlene, she was the one that made the decisions to take those awful drugs. She was the one that was weak minded and fell into the hands of Douglass and group. I have to say I'm a very strong person and you know what I will not let anything or anybody let me think otherwise.

Well Diary, till next time, I love you, thanks for being patient with me. You will always be my very, very best friend.

Kim.

I wrote on a piece of paper as The Queen had destroyed my Diary beyond repair.

Chapter 15
Transformation

Yesterday I saw a girl I had the utmost respect for run into the busy street outside my home and lose her ability to walk. This was a person I thought had all the right ingredients to succeed. This was a girl I was sure to envy in twenty years. It amazed me how she could have ruined her life over some stupid drugs. I felt so bad about the accident to the point I blamed myself. I thought to myself over and over again that I should have never opened the door, especially with Darlene in the state she was in. I should have made her lay down and go to sleep or I should have locked her in the basement closet. I don't know, there must have been something I could have done. I really hated myself for being so stupid.

It was a gloomy, cloudy day that May 1, 1968 and it was just the right ambience for my somber mood. After spending most of the night wide awake and most of the morning changing diapers, I decided I had had enough of my homeless home, so I closed my last diaper and handed my little sister to her rightful mother.

"What are you giving me this child for?" The Queen asked.

"Because I'm not the one who spit her out?" I said shivering in my boots.

"What, who the hell do you think you are talking to?"

"You, who else?" I Said ready to run for my life.

"Girl go outside and get me a switch off that big ass tree."

"Hell no. If you want a switch then you get it yourself." I said opening the front door.

"I just know you're not leaving this house when I have places to go." The Queen angrily said as my baby sister began crying.

"Yep." I said waiting for the chairs to start flying while quickly making my way out the house. Wow, I couldn't believe my defiance of The Queen. It made me feel so strong and grown up, yet I felt so bad for disrespecting the woman who gave me life.

As I walked down Preston Street towards downtown, I realized there was a better way of letting out my anger other than to lash out at the Queen.

"I should have had more respect for her, I should have been more obedient. Oh well, maybe I'll apologize when I get back or maybe I won't apologize when I get back." I thought to myself as I walked along.

As I aimlessly walked through the crowded city streets to an unknown destination I couldn't help think about Darlene's accident. Concentrating on her, I was completely unaware that I had entered an area I would have normally avoided. It was an area known for its high drunk population, old boarded up store fronts, homeless old men and wanna be prostitutes. I had no idea as to how that part of town deteriorated to such a state as just a few years earlier us kids use to play at the park across the street while our parents shopped.

"Hey little girl, I'll give some of my stuff for some of yours", One old drunk said stumbling toward me when my conscious mind took over from my unconscious mind.

"Get away from me you old drunk" I replied angrily.

Ignoring my command, the drunk continued toward me. With him came the stench of years of stale cigarettes, high concentrations of alcohol and the funk from years of not bathing. The odors were so bad that the closer he came the more my stomach squeezed; and the closer he came the higher the acid levels in my throat seem to multiply. By the time he came within two feet of me I swore my stomach had made its way up my throat and had mixed with billions of particles of acid which were now ready to launch like a rocket through my mouth. Seemed to be a constant theme with me.

"Come on little girl, this stuff's good." He said holding up his bottle of Old Grand Dad.

Realizing that this teeth-less, dirt caked, nappy hair drunk didn't deserve an answer I angrily pushed him aside and bolted forward to notice a young girl, no older than myself, laying in the street about a foot away from a nearby sore hole. As the girl turned from her right side to her back her eyes rolled back in her head and what was left of her last meal was slowly expelling from her mouth and onto the street. As the girl lay helplessly on the cold ground passerbys and the news media looked curiously on but were reluctant to assist.

It was amazing how people could see a girl obviously distressed and not help. And the news media, just after a story, was so insensitive to her condition that they just continued filming as she continued to throw up a food and blood mixture.

"Why doesn't somebody help this girl?" I yelled to the crowd.

"Why should we?" A man asked.

"Hey, she got herself in this situation, she should know how to get herself out of it." He nonchalantly continued.

Upset over the situation I made my way to the girl and sat her up against the curve. After cleaning the girl's face with a tissue, I panned the many faces of the crowd for any signs of reaction.

"Just what kind of people are you?" I screamed louder.

"Little girl", The news reporter said.

"Just what is your relationship to this girl?" The reporter continued.

With the stupid question asked by the news reporter my once high opinion of man dwindled into nothing. Attempting to help the girl, I tried aimlessly to drag her from the cold street. After several minutes, I realized that I didn't have the strength to move her, as she weighed some thirty pounds more than I. But I wouldn't give up so I pulled and pulled for several more minutes with no luck. Then suddenly as tears uncontrollably rolled from my eyes a tall, dignified man walked to the girl and easily lifted her off the ground. As the clouds of my tears cleared, I noticed that the man was Mr. Parkinson. Despite my recent resentment for him I knew everything would be okay.

&

Moments later Mr. Parkinson, carrying the girl, and I arrived at his store and he sits her on a chair in his office. After calling for an ambulance he makes the girl comfortable by putting a blanket over her cold body. At some point her body showed fewer signs of alcohol abuse and displayed more signs of sleeping. After the ambulance arrives and takes the girl to the hospital Mr. Parkinston shakes his head then takes a seat behind his desk. Ready to take this opportunity to lay him out about not telling me that he was my father, I suddenly took a deep breath and began to speak.

"Kimberly, you're my daughter" He suddenly spoke softly.

Shocked at his confession I just sat there. I didn't know what to do or what to say. I felt like giving him the tightest hug possible but on the other hand I felt like hitting him for waiting so long to tell me.

"I wanted to tell you for such a long time, but circumstances prevented me from doing so." He said.

"I don't get it, why couldn't you tell me."

"Well" He said.

"At the time your mother became pregnant with you I was married with two small children. I loved your mother and even today I still have very strong feelings for her. But at the time your mother and I decided it was best if we did not announce that you were my daughter considering I was married and your mother was engaged to Freddie Day."

"My mother was going to marry Freddie?" I asked.

"Yes, they were very close and in fact, back then they were perfect for each other." Mr. Parkinston answered.

"I don't get it, if she loved Freddie so much and you loved your wife how did you get together and have me?"

"It was just something that happened. We were really good friends and one night while Freddie was in the Army the two of us were out with a few friends. We had been drinking and later that night it happened."

"I guess I shouldn't be surprised, I mean my mother's the same way now." I said.

"Don't be so hard on your mother, she really is trying hard."

I know she has done some questionable things during your short life but she does love you kids." He said.

"Naomi said the same thing."

"And Naomi is correct."

"You know Kim. When I saw you out there trying to help that girl I almost cried. I was so proud to be your father. I wanted to let the world know that my daughter cared about people and that she's a special young lady. But I couldn't do that without first telling you. Kim, is it okay that I let the world know that you're my daughter, that you're my baby?" He said as a tear or two formed in his eyes.

"Yes!" I said after a long split-second thought.

Chapter 16

Accusations

That night I had trouble sleeping because I couldn't help think about knowing who my father was. Finally, my dream of having a father like Mr. Parkinston was real; that is Mr. Parkinston was my father. During the night, I purposely hesitated to fall asleep because I didn't want to wake up and find out that finding my father was only a dream. I didn't want that feeling of elation to dissipate with the closing of my eyes so I struggled to exhaustion to keep them open. But with the passing of every minute the weight of my eye-lids grew heavier and by the time I knew it I had drifted off into dream world. But to my joy Mr. Parkinston was still my father when I woke up that next day.

One would think that finally knowing my father would keep me smiling but with Darlene's accident in the back of my mind it was hard to focus on the joyous news. Like Kevin Darlene was still hospitalized but unlike Kevin Darlene was wide awake and talking. A few people from church visited her the day after the accident and later reported to the congregation that she was doing fine and that her spirits were high. Up to that day I had resisted the temptation to visit her for fear of breaking down and collapsing into tears.

While sitting in church one Sunday I couldn't help think about Darlene. Like every day since the accident I couldn't focus on anything except that horrible day. The guilt was getting to me so I knew I couldn't wait any longer to visit her. So, that day after visiting Kevin I built up enough nerve to visit my friend. Conveniently she was in the same hospital as Kevin, just on a lower floor. As I approached her room I stopped and took several deep breaths before entering.

"Good afternoon Mr. And Mrs. Montgomery. Hi Darlene." I cautiously said approaching Darlene's bed.

"Hi Kim!" Darlene happily said.

Relieved to see that indeed Darlene's spirits were high, I approached the oversized bed, sat on the side and gave her as bear hug.

"Oh I missed you so much." I cried.

"I missed you too. How come you haven't visited before?"

"Because I was scared and I blamed myself for what happened."

"It wasn't your fault."

"But I still blame myself."

"Well don't worry, the doctor said that I will be able to walk again. He said it will be awhile but I won't have to spend the rest of my life in a wheelchair."

"Really? That's great."

"Really." Darlene replied.

Darlene and I gave each other another long bear hug as we

wiped tears from each other's eyes.

"You know what?" I said

"I have a feeling you'll be doing Double Dutch in no time. And next year our team will be going to the city championships and you will be with us." I cried.

"You think so?" She asked.

"Yeah, I think so."

Darlene's parents seem less than enthusiastic about our long-term plans. As a matter of fact, they were quiet during my entire visit. After forty minutes of girly giggles we said our good-byes and I promised to visit her every day until she went home.

"Kimberly I'll walk you to the elevators." Mrs. Montgomery said.

"Okay, thank you." I replied.

Mrs. Montgomery and I quietly made our way to the elevators and together waited amongst a large group of silent guests.

"Kimberly, I don't want you to come here again." Mrs. Montgomery said

"Why?"

"Because not only are you a bad influence of Darlene, it's because of you that she's here."

"But Mrs. Montgomery I tried to stop her from running into the street."

"No, little girl I mean it's because of you that my child took those damn drugs in the first place." Mrs. Montgomery said raising her voice.

"I don't get it." I replied.

"I know all about your adventure with those drugs and your

sex episode with that drug attic. Darlene told me everything."

"But Mrs. Montgomery."

"But nothing. I know Darlene took those drugs because you wanted her to."

"No, I didn't know anything about it until she came to my house that day."

"Don't lie to me."

"But.."

"But nothing, you and your ghetto family will be paid a visit by the Police, so if I were you, I would clean my house of all those drugs and hope you don't miss anything." She said before heading back to Darlene's room.

That conversation not only upset me it embarrassed me as the crowd waiting for the elevator over heard the entire thing. I just wanted to cry or hide under a rock or something. I didn't want to ride in the same elevator as those people who I figured had labeled me a junky by that time. But, after the experiences of the past several months I refused to let Mrs. Montgomery's comments degrade me so I put my head up high, continued to wait until the elevator came, rode down with the crowd then confidently walked out with them.

Later that evening as my mother and I played with Mae and Naomi cleaned the kitchen of the dinner dishes a knock was heard at the door.

"I'll get it." My mother said before walking to the door.

After carefully opening the door she revealed Mrs. Montgomery standing with a face so angry it could have scared the nose off the wicked witch of the West.

"Good evening Cynthia." My mother said before Mrs. Montgomery barged her way in.

"How's Darlene?" My mother asked shocked at her

behavior.

"Look" Mrs. Montgomery angrily said.

"I'm here about that daughter of yours." She finished.

"Well, which one. I do have five you know."

"That one." She said angrily pointing to me.

"Excuse me, what kind of problem do you have with Kim?" The Queen asked.

"Your daughter was the one who gave my baby those damn drugs that landed her in that hospital."

"Lady, you are out of your fuckin' mind." The Queen angrily said.

"Oh no I'm not. Just ask your little drug attic daughter."

"Mommy, I didn't give Darlene those drugs, she came here high. The only thing I tried to do was help her." I said.

"You lying little girl." Mrs. Montgomery said.

"But it's the truth." I insisted.

"Look Bitch, if my daughter tells me it's the truth then I know it's true. So why don't you take your ugly black ass out of my house before I make sure your life is dependent on drugs to keep it goin'."

"If you touch me, I swear I'll have all you low life's thrown in jail."

"Mommy she thinks that I gave Darlene drugs because Douglass talked me into taking some of that stuff a few weeks ago." I said to The Queen.

A few moments of silence rang out as my mother slowly digested my comment. As that annoying clock loudly ticked away the seconds my mother's face turned as red as a fire engine. Then true to form she shrugged her large shoulders then angrily looked at me with her silver dollar sized brownish black eyes.

"Oh no." I thought to myself.

"The Queen is back." My thoughts continued.

"Douglass!" She screamed staring at me.

The house once again became silent except again for that annoyingly clock. To prevent The Queen's eyes from popping out of her head we all remained still. No one person moved a muscle, not one sniffle was heard. Minutes later, Douglass casually makes his way to the top of the stairs, unaware of the brewing pot at the bottom.

"Get down here!" She yelled realizing Douglass' presence.

Aware of the possible repercussions of deliberately disobeying the Queen Douglass quickly runs down the steps and stood innocently next to her.

"What the hell did you do to my child?"

"Who?" Douglass asked.

"You talked my child into taking some of those damn drugs you and your sorry ass attic friends inhale."

Stunned by her comment Douglass stood quietly as if deciding whether to protect himself by lying or protect me by telling the truth. After looking at the floor, then looking at me, then backing away from the Queen he raised his head, stared at the Queen then closed his eyes.

"Yes ma'am, I did." He admitted to my surprise.

"Why would you do that to her, you know she has a hard time saying no, especially to us."

"I don't know, I don't know." Douglass said opening his eyes.

Upset over his actions my mother instantly took her right hand and slapped it across the right side of Douglass' face.

"Don't you ever go near by child again with that damn stuff, is that clear." She said staring Douglass down. The Queen then turns her big hips toward me followed her large eyes.

"Kimberly, if he ever tries to talk you into taking that shit again you better let me know. Because I swear, I'll kick his ass out of here." She continued.

"Mommy, you don't have to worry I'll never let that happen again."

Pleasantly shocked at my comment she gave me a quick smile then tended to the business of the moment. Meanwhile Mrs. Montgomery was not moved by the family bonding. Her face now complimented my mothers and her hands were now attempting to find a hidden position to prevent from hitting someone.

"So" she said.

"You ghetto dwellers think it's okay for this sorry excuse for a girl to give my baby drugs." She continued.

"But I didn't give Darlene any drugs. I would never do something like that to her."

"Look you little lying drug attic. You may have your slut mother convinced that you are so innocent but..."

Blood boiling in my mother's body to the point of eruption, she quickly walked to Mrs. Montgomery, takes her right hand and begins to plants a good one across Mrs. Montgomery's narrow face. But before my mother's hand approached Mrs. Montgomery's face Douglass grabs it and steps between the two.

"Stop it, it was my fault. I gave Darlene the drugs. I got her addicted." Douglass explained.

"What?" Mrs. Montgomery said.

"I knew Darlene had a crush on me, so I took advantage of

it. I also had her stealing money from the gang."

Realizing Douglass was telling the truth Mrs. Montgomery took a few steps backward and began crying.

"I always thought I had control of my child. I had no idea she could get away from me long enough to do those things. I guess I failed as a mother."

"Are you out of your mind." My mother said.

"How in the hell do you think you can control everything that goes on with your child. Shit if I blamed myself for everything my kids did, I would have called it quits a long time ago.

Mrs. Montgomery tears slowly turned to a few chuckles as she interpreted my mother's comments. She then stared aimlessly at our small group and shakes her head.

"Delores you may except your children's actions but I don't. I swear I will make sure you people pay for what happened to my daughter." She said before calmly walking out.

My mother, convinced that her motherly duties for the day were over headed upstairs, leaving Mae on the living room chair. Meanwhile Naomi began sweeping the kitchen floor as if nothing had happened. Still angry at Douglass I quietly walked to the couch, turned on the television, quietly began flipping channels and stopping at a channel playing my favorite show *The Twilight Zone*. Before engrossing myself in the show my anger for Douglass took hold of me so I jumped off the couch, raced to Naomi, grab the broom from her hands and knocked it over Douglass' head.

"You idiot, you idiot. I hate you. Don't you ever come near me and Darlene again. I don't care whether you are dying or something horrible I don't ever want to talk to you again." I yelled.

Chapter 17

Return of My Best Friend

Two days had passed since Mrs. Montgomery's visit. Kevin began to improve as he actually moved one hand and slowly turned his head toward the sound of our voices. I knew it wasn't the Hollywood miracle but it gave me a since of hope.

It had been several weeks since my mother tore apart my Diary but for some reason that day, I felt lonelier and more depressed than normal. I didn't have anyone to confide in, no one to listen to me complain and no one to just be friends with. My Diary meant the world to me. No person, no animal, no other Diary could have replaced it. We had a bond that couldn't be replicated, we had a bond that only the two of us understood.

As I lay in bed looking at the torn pages of my Diary, I tried thinking of everything I could to bring my best friend back to life. Excited at the thought of having my friend back I quickly jumped out of bed and gathered tape, an empty three ring binder and the scattered pages of the diary. Feeling like a surgeon I tried several methods of putting my friend back together. After several hours of taping, un-taping, and re-taping the Diary was in no better shape than when I started.

Frustrated at the thought of never talking to my Best Friend again I threw the pages and the useless materials around the room and began crying. Suddenly after two buckets of water poured down my cheeks I came up with the greatest idea, so I quickly got up and went to the drawer in which I kept all those gifts I didn't want but didn't feel like throwing away.

Buried in the bottom of the drawer I found a Diary given to me by of all people, The Queen. Yes, that's true, The Queen gave it to me on my twelfth birthday. It was much nicer and larger than my torn-up Best Friend, it was just that it wasn't my Best friend. But I figured out a way to deal with that issue. I decided to copy all the pages from the old Diary to this one. It was just like a person changing their clothes. I mean, despite what you wear you are still the same person inside, right? Excited over the return of my Best friend I spent the next three hours organizing the paper pieces and copying the entries from the old Diary to the new one.

Dear Diary,

April 20, 1968

> *I'm so happy to have you back. It's been really lonely without you. Without you to talk to the days have been long and sleep has been non-existent. I missed you, I missed you, I missed you and I will never let anyone hurt you again. Diary you will always stay close to me and if anybody even attempts to get their hands on you again they will suffer the same fate as Dr. King.*

> *Thank God not much has happened since we last spoke. Even though Kevin is still in the hospital I'm blessed that he is still alive. There hasn't been much change but we still have him. I've prayed every night for him to recover but so far God has not listened. I guess he's too busy with the rest of the world's problems to deal with my request.*

> *I still haven't received the scholarship test results but my teacher said that they would be mailed sometime this week. Diary, lately I've just had this sinking feeling that I did not get the scholarship.*

> *Diary, I was going to tell you this later but I can't wait. Diary, The Queen told me that Mr. Parkinston is my father and Mr. Parkinston confirmed it. I'm so happy to have a father. Now that you are back and with me knowing my father, I feel life is getting better. Thank God for that. But I want Kevin back also.*

"Kim", Naomi said entering the room and interrupting.

"Yeah", I said putting the pen in my Diary at the page I was currently writing.

"The letter you have been waiting for is here" she said handing me a letter size envelope.

"Thanks." I said snatching the letter from Naomi.

The moment of truth had arrived, the scholarship results were now in. Opening that letter meant the possibility of my dreams dying forever or the possibility of my dreams coming true. I knew at that point I wanted complete privacy as I opened the letter, so I ran into the tiny bathroom I shared with the entire family. I immediately closed the door upon entering and sat on the side of the tub.

I must have stared at the envelope for thirty minutes before getting the nerve to open it. Finally, after doing everything to avoid opening the letter I slowly tore a hole in the left side of it. Eventually after meticulously tearing a hole large enough to remove the letter I picked it up and sat there several more minutes. Finally, I opened the letter.

&

Dear Diary,

I'm sorry I didn't end our last conversation in my normal manner but Naomi came in the room and handed me the letter about the scholarship. I scored a 99% out of 100% on the Math, Verbal and Grammar parts and scored a 98% on the history part. I also did amazingly well on the writing part scoring a 149 out of 150. I'm so proud of myself, even though I didn't get the scholarship. I don't know why I wasn't selected, maybe somebody scored higher than I did or maybe it was all the shit going on in this sorry excuse for a family. No private school would want a kid like me. Gosh, I wouldn't be surprised if Mrs. Montgomery had something to do with me not getting it. Shit she probably told them that I would be a bad influence on those preppy little white girls. Well I don't care; they can take their little rich girls and throw them all into the Harbor for all I care. It doesn't matter anyway, it's all over as far as I'm concerned.

Well Diary, I'm too depressed to continue right now, I just wanna' fade away. Talk to you later, if not, have a good life.
Kim

Chapter 18

A Complete Image

April showers had somewhere given way to May flowers, but not in my concrete jungle. Even before the riots of early April converted Pennsylvania Avenue into an abandoned war zone the only green we ever saw on the ground were pieces of broken green bottles. Oh, I'm mistaken, we also saw tons of torn papers, some of which were green, and tons of tiny little green bugs crawling into every little crevasse they could find. You know, I could never figure out why any living creature would want to come into the ghetto when most others were trying to get out. But I had to give it to the bold sun-of-a-guns, they had nerve.

Despite the less than pleasant outdoor conditions life in Western Baltimore City really wasn't all that bad. I mean, besides the litter, the green bugs and the intermitted drunks I somehow managed to make it to the ripe old age of fourteen even though there were many days I felt as thou life outside was easier than life inside of my "Home Sweet Home".

Outside you could easily clean up the broken bottles to avoid accidentally cutting yourself. Or you could quickly cross the street to avoid a drunk or two or three and to think about it, you could shoo away a few green bugs. But inside the confines of my humble abode I was bound by the actions of others, who, like me, were confined to the same dark closed-in space. This small space forced us to share in each other's grief, mischief, sorrow and hell. Our lives, though physically separate emotionally created a web of continuous conflict.

The residents that shared this space seem to take on a maze of interlocking pieces of a complex puzzle. This puzzle, whose jagged pieces appeared difficult to connect somehow managed to interlock. Like this puzzle, if there's one missing piece it's difficult to see a complete image. Physically our puzzle lacked a small piece we called Kevin. Emotionally that missing piece had prevented the rest of the pieces from connecting, especially me.

From the night Kevin was shot to that May Day my thoughts were almost solely focused on him. Between Kevin and Darlene, I couldn't focus on school, I couldn't focus on home, my dysfunctional family, nothing! All I wanted was for the person I loved the most to wake up. I worried each time he struggled to breath, I worried each time he had a seizure and I cried each time his heart stopped.

In my mind that missing puzzle piece would never be found, that there would forever remain a hole in the image. To me, it was just a matter of time before the final words of confirmation rang in our ears.

But, to my delight that never happened. That early May Day proved to be the best day of my life. As my mother straighten my hair, and Naomi and Beatrice ate dinner a knock was heard at the door.

"Ouch" I said ducking my head after my mother accidentally burns my scalp with the hot comb.

"Oh Kimberly that didn't hurt." My mother commented.

"Yes it did." I cried.

"Well, since you think it hurts so much you just sit there and cry while I answer the door." She said before heading toward the door.

After opening the wore out door the Queen found Mrs. Wilson on the other side.

"Good afternoon Delores", Mrs. Wilson said smiling as she entered.

"Hey" Mrs. Wilson said as she made her way pass the Queen and walks toward the kitchen.

"Troubles here." My mother said following behind her.

"Old Delores, shut up." Mrs. Wilson replied.

"You know, you two act just like sisters." Naomi said.

"Hey who knows, with the way we multiply around this place you never know." My mother said.

"I tell you." Mrs. Wilson said staring at the Queen.

"Oh hush it up." The Queen smartly said.

"Delores, when are you going to take down that black sock hanging on your door, the riots have been over with for weeks." Mrs. Wilson asked.

"When I get good and ready to." The Queen replied.

"I don't know why I even asked you that question, when I knew the answer." Mrs. Wilson said looking at me as the Queen continued to straighten my hair.

"But look, I just got a call from Douglass, he's at the

hospital" She continued.

"Oh my God, is Kevin still alive?" Naomi asked.

"As a matter of fact, yes. He's awake and asking for you guys."

"I knew it, I just knew God would take care of him. Oh thank you, thank you, thank you." Naomi cried out loud.

The news of Kevin's recovery had the family screaming and dancing. It was like a bunch of ten-year-olds coming downstairs on Christmas morning to discover a boat load of toys. It was then that I realized our image would be whole once again.

Immediately after the cheers subsided the family raced to the hospital and by God's great will Kevin was sitting up laughing and talking to Douglass. Like always, Douglass had a way of making a person laugh, even when they were ready to kill him. At that instance, I realized life goes on and as pastor Hemmings always said "Forgive your fellow man as he will one day repent his sins." Though I will never forget what Douglass did I forgave him that day.

Five days later Dr. Holmes was ready to release Kevin as the nurses had a hard time keeping him in bed. It was as if his fairy God Mother pointed her magic wand at him and chanted "You will wake up and return to your old self." And that he did.

To prepare for Kevin's return the family spent that evening cleaning and decorating our small home. Kathy and I made a long banner made of taped notebook paper reading "Welcome Home Kevin." Douglass decorated the room he and Kevin shared with posters of the King of Soul and borrowed a record player from Mrs. Wilson so Kevin could listen to his favorite singer while recuperating in bed.

My mother cooked several of Kevin's favorite dishes including Macaroni and cheese, fried fish and string beans. Beatrice, our professional student, gathered all the work Kevin missed and placed them next to his bed with a note reading "Make-up classes start promptly at 4:00 p.m. Tuesday."

Man, I couldn't believe it, this was the first time I was able to take the "dys" out of dysfunctional when referring to my family.

By the time midnight approached our energy had depleted. After hanging the last poster and cooking the last dish we all headed upstairs for the night. Moments before going to bed Naomi, Kathy, Beatrice and I kneeled down at the front window for a moment of prayer. As Naomi thanked God for allowing Kevin to re-join our family the rest of us listened intensely. Immediately following, we all settled down for the night knowing that all was well.

&

"Help!!" A loud scream was heard from my mother's room around 2 a.m. that night.

"Help!!" Another scream was heard followed by the sounds of breaking glass.

Startled by the sudden screams my sisters and I quickly hopped out of bed and ran toward my mother's room. As the screams continued the smell of smoke filled the air. As we approached my mother's room, we noticed Douglass trying to open the door but struggling as flames protruded from the cracks between the door and the doorframe.

"Help!!" My mother screamed again but with more intensity.

"We're trying Mom, we're trying" I yelled.

"The flames are everywhere." I heard her scream before silence.

"Mom" Beatrice yelled. But there was no response.

"Somebody get a hammer!" Douglass ordered.

As ordered, I ran down the dark stairs and into the kitchen to search the junk drawer for the sole hammer in which we own. As I rummaged through the small drawer, whose front had been missing for months, I notice flames descending from my mother's room just above the kitchen.

"Douglass, fire is comin' in the kitchen!" I screamed as I finally located the hammer.

"Hurray up with that hammer. I need to get Mom out of there." He ordered screaming.

After taking a quick look at the spreading flames I ran upstairs and handed the hammer to Douglass.

"Now yall git out of here." He said after taking the hammer.

"No, we have to help you get Mom out of there." Beatrice yelled.

"I said git out of here." Douglass angrily repeated.

"Come on, let's go to Mrs. Wilson's and call the fire department." Naomi said trying to calm Beatrice down.

"I don't want to go. I gotta make sure Mom is okay." I screamed as Douglass finally opened the door to reveal a wall of flames.

"Kim, come on, let Douglass do what he has to do." Kathy yelled over the sounds of the roaring flames.

Naomi, barely digesting my last cry, grabbed my left arm and dragged me down the steps and toward the front door. Before the walls of the stairwell prevented me from seeing the door to my mother's room, I noticed Douglass entering the fiery smoke-filled room. As we reached the front door, we noticed flames engulfing the kitchen and smoke had begun filling the living room. Suddenly the kitchen ceiling crashed down carrying several large pieces of furniture.

"Douglass, please hurray up, please!" I yelled before Naomi pulled me out the door.

Several seconds later we arrived at Mrs. Wilson's house and began hysterically banging on her front door.

"Mrs. Wilson, Mrs. Wilson please answer the door, please." I screamed begging as my sisters tried repeatedly to calm me down. Suddenly the door opens and we all run into her dark home.

"What's going on?" Mrs. Wilson said.

"You gotta call the fire department. Our house, it's burning down, you gotta call now." Naomi said.

"Oh my God." Mrs. Wilson responded.

"My mother and Douglass, they're still in the house. There're gonna die." I yelled.

"Kimberly calm down, everything's going to be okay." Mrs. Wilson said as she dialed the fire department.

Eyes glued to our scared faces; Mrs. Wilson pondered as to what to say after hanging up the phone.

"They're on the way" She started.

"Everything will be okay." She finished trying to convince herself and us.

The room remained silent for several minutes as we all stood frozen. Not a word was spoken, not a muscle moved. It was as though time had stood still. Consciously I had no recollection of that time, life just passed me by. The only blessing in that whole thing was that Mae was with Uncle Marvin and Kevin wasn't coming home until the next day.

Finally, the sound of sirens brought me back from no man's land.

"Thank God" A voice said as I ran to the front door.

"Kimberly, stay here." Mrs. Wilson yelled.

"No" I replied as I ran out the door and down the steps.

Trying to stop me from returning home my sisters and Mrs. Wilson began to run and catch me but being much younger I was way too fast. As I approached the engulfed house, I noticed several firemen attempting to enter.

"Thank you" I said to myself.

"Thank you." I repeated.

"All will be okay." I thought to myself before realizing flames were coming out of the windows of the bedroom I shared with my sisters.

As a crowd of on lookers gathered, I wondered when that bad dream would end. I wanted to see my mother and oldest brother, just when would my life be normal.

"No!" I suddenly screamed. "No!" I screamed hysterically again when I realized that my very best friend was still in the room that was now over taken by flames. Losing it again was not an option so without thought I ran through the crowd and headed into the burning house.

"Hey little girl, don't go in there." I faintly heard someone say.

"Kim, come back" Naomi screamed as I entered the dark smoky burning house.

The house, just hours before, we had decorated so nicely for Kevin's home coming was slowly becoming a pile of rubble. There were bright red flames climbing every wall in the kitchen and every piece of living room furniture was covered with soot. The staircase that normally stood out like the nose on Pinocchio's face was now invisible.

Determined to rescue my best friend, I had to somehow find the staircase and make my way upstairs. So, like a blind man I ran my hands along the wall to the left of the entry door and located the stairs. Ignoring the orders of the firemen to leave the building I made contact with the hot medal banister and enduring the pain started up the dark stairwell.

"Little girl, don't go up there." A fireman screamed attempting to catch up with me.

Hands blistering, eyes burning and coughing hysterically I slowly made my way to the top of the stairs. Realizing that the firemen were getting closer I picked up the pace to reach my room. Unfamiliar to me, I was now forced to contemplate every step. Not realizing exactly where I was panic set in causing me to stop in my tracks. Instantly, my eyes teared from the thick smoke. I lost focus, but I knew I had put myself in this situation to save my best friend.

Suddenly, just seconds before the firemen reached the top of the stairs the smoke cleared and with that my focus returned. At that point I could see the dresser drawer in which I kept my best friend. For some reason, flames had not touched the old wooded and bruised piece of furniture. Like a lion dodging its prey I quickly ran into the room and retrieved my diary from the top drawer. Excited with my accomplishment I headed toward the door just as a fireman caught up with me.

"Young lady, did you hear us calling you?" He said.

"Yes sir, but I just had to get this." I said showing him my best friend.

"Well you need to get out of here so we can put out this fire." He continued as two other firemen started putting out the flames in the bedroom.

"Please sir, don't let our house burn down." I cried.

"We can't do that with you in here. Now let's get you out of here." The gentle firemen said before somehow managing to pick up my hundred-pound body and then carrying me down the stairs and out the door to Mrs. Wilson and my waiting sisters.

"Now you stay out here." He said with care.

"Yes sir." I said amazed that such a strong tough man could be so gentle.

An hour later the fire was completely out. But we still had not seen Douglass nor my mother.

"Hey, did you see my mother and brother in there?" Beatrice asked of one of the firemen as he began preparing to leave.

"Yeah, your mother is in the back yard and I'm sorry to tell you that I don't think your brother made it." He said.

"Oh" She said stunned.

"No!!!" Kathy screamed to the top of her lungs.

"NO!!!!!!!!!!!!!!!" I screamed as I began backing away from the group, my eyes watering and my right hand now throbbing violently beyond tolerance.

And now knowing that Douglass was dead because of all my wishes and cries to send him to the cornfields I was also in a massive state of panic. The more I thought about the night's events the more panic took over and the more panic took over the faster my backward movements became quick gallops.

"He's with God now." Naomi said hugging Kathy.

"I hate this world, I wanna kill myself, I can't take it!!!" I yelled flustered.

"Kim, calm down." Mrs. Wilson said.

"This world sucks, I hate it, I hate it, I hate it." I continued ignoring Mrs. Wilson.

"Kim, everything will be okay." Mrs. Wilson continued.

"No it won't be. Every time I think that life is getting better it just gets worse. And it's goin' to get worse and worse and worse." I screamed.

"No it's not." Mrs. Wilson replied.

"Kimberly things will get better. Things happen for a reason." Naomi said.

"The Hell with this damn life. The hell with all of you, the hell with this damn world." I screamed turning away from the group and quickly running away.

"Kimberly, come back here." I heard Mrs. Wilson say.

"Let her go. She just has to calm down." Naomi insisted.

&

Dear Diary,

Douglass is dead, he's dead and it's my fault. Diary I should have never wished him to die or to the cornfields. It's my fault. I hate myself. I don't deserve to live. I knew I should have ended it when I had the chance, I knew it.

Me!!!

&

I said crying to my best friend two hours later as I sat on a cold bench in Druid Hill Park some six miles from my home. Unable to finish my conversation because the park light just above the bench in which I was sitting went out I closed my diary and began crying even harder. At that point I found myself staring into the vast darkness of the empty park. That was the first time ever I had been alone, outside, cold in the dark of the night. It was scary, it was black and it was lonely. I never knew the quiet of the night could be so loud and the dark of the night could be so visible.

Sitting on the old wooden bench and staring aimlessly into the dark I waited for a creature of some sort to suddenly appear and snatch me. To some extent I was ready for something to take me to the same place as Douglass. Patiently I waited and waited and waited until finally the dark of night turned into the light of a new day. The daylight emphasized that "yes my life was not easy" and "yes my future was uncertain" and "yes I'm not one of the fortunate ones."

As daylight settled in I was once again able to talk to my Best Friend. Unsure of what to say I began reading over the last few months of entries. Reading them made me realize that yes indeed "my life was hard" and "Yes indeed" I was not one of the fortunate ones" and "yes indeed my future was uncertain". But they also made me realize that life as I perceived it was somewhat twisted then the way things really were.

Though I always labeled my family as dysfunctional they were really just pieces of that complex puzzle trying to find their place on the collaborated image. It was as if someone shook up the box of pieces, poured them on a table and prayed that all the pieces were present to form a perfect image. Before the fire, I could see that all the pieces were declared present and the image was also declared perfect. Now we're permanently missing a piece, a piece who started with a peeled edge but later was fixed with the peeled edge glued to its cardboard backing.

That piece had become a strong contribution to the image. It slowly provided the framework for holding the remaining pieces together. Thought that piece was gone it would never be forgotten and I knew in my heart there was nothing I could do about it. The absence of that piece lied on my shoulders and because of that I knew the image would never be whole again. I couldn't face the consequences of my actions and thoughts. I couldn't return home and I couldn't go on living with the guilt, so like my mother's mother I decided disappearance was the only way to cope.

Some three hours after daylight, I found myself standing on the corner of Park Heights Ave. and Coldspring Lane hungry and tired. As the endless parade of people walked aimlessly by my thoughts of joining Douglass intensified. Instinctively I knew I had to find some sort of nourishment but on the other hand I knew starving to death was an easy way of ending things.

"Hey, look who it is." I heard a voice say from behind.

Ignoring the voice, I began quickly walking away toward Resistertown Rd.

"Hey Kim, its me." The voice said.

Realizing the voice sounded familiar I stopped, turned around and noticed a tall slender raggedy dressed man standing and smiling. It was him, the bleeder.

"Where you goin'?" He asked.

"None of your business, so just leave me the hell alone."

"Ah come on Kim, why you actin' like this."

"I said leave me alone you drug sniffing nose bleedin' horny ugly nappy hair ass-hole."

"Ah, I didn't do anything to you, why you hate me."

"You're so damn stupid."

"Hey what you talkin' about I made it to the tenth grade." The Bleeder bragged.

"Oh, I'm so impressed." I said unimpressed.

"You know, I thought you were a nice girl, but you're just as trashy as these other little whores around here."

"Yeah, thanks to you."

"What the hell you talkin' bout."

"You bastard, you know what you did to me. Dam-it you had your way with me when you knew I couldn't fight you back."

"Ah hell little girl, I wish I did, but who wanted to do it with a screaming little girl. And not to mention that Douglass came back in and dragged me out of there."

Digesting what the bleeder just said I became speechless after realizing that thank God I didn't lose my virginity that awful day. If it weren't for the fact that I hated that ugly goofball I would have given him the tightest hug of his life. But instead I slowly smiled then walked away.

"Ah, where you goin'?" He asked.

"Like I said, none of your business."

"Oh, just go away. I can't stand you anyway." He finished disgusted.

"Well good, the feeling's mutual."

Three days later I found myself still wondering around Druid Hill Park. I was determined never to return to my family and I was determined to limit my remaining days. Though I was attempting to starve to death I found it hard to ignore the intense hunger pains so I often found scraps of food left in trash cans and on the grounds of the well-attended park.

During the day, it was hard to find a place to go to the bathroom as the park was busy with visiting school groups, families and lovers. After carefully searching the entire park I found a place behind a bush next to the reptile house to use as an Outhouse. It wasn't the most pleasant place to do my business due to the endless bugs and large patches of poison Ivy, but it was the most private. At times nature seem to invade my commode as there were several times I waited more than twenty minutes as groups of about seventy worms burrowed their way into the ground. When I finally got a chance to do what needed to be done, I found it uneasy and hard to relax for fear that the worms would make their way out of the hole and up my butt.

Of course, those times seemed like the longest times I had ever spent waiting for Mother Nature to go to work, if I only had a newspaper. At night, the lights from the conservatory made sleeping on a nearby bench an ideal place. Not only was it well-lit, it was also hidden from passing cars and walker byes. To make the bench more comfortable I stole blankets and a pillow from a group of picnickers. It wasn't the bed I shared with Kathy but it was the best I could do.

As the days passed, my right hand blistered, covering every inch from the palm to the tips of my middle finger. At times, thick rankly smelling liquid slowly leaked from every blood and puss filled pebble sized formation.

The next couple of weeks were spent dodging visitors, raiding trashcans and wondering the park. I had no idea of the day of the week or even the time of the day. Though I didn't know for sure, my weight seems to have gone from a normal one-hundred to no more than eighty pounds. I knew that it was just a matter of time before the end. I had become so weak that I could barely walk the short distance between the Reptile House and the Conservatory.

Eventually, my bathroom moved to a tree some ten feet away from my bed. As the days passed the smell of my decaying waste concentrated the air to the point where even the birds refused to visit.

Me personally, at that point, could care less. I was tired and ready to meet my maker. I was to the point where I could easily go a day without eating and I could easily go a day without going to the bathroom. I hadn't spoken to another sole since the day after the fire and it bothered me that my last words were spoken to that stupid ass bleeder. But even though it bothered me at least I found out the truth about that awful day. I was ready to join Douglass and Marcus and I was ready to face the Gods at the Pearly gates. But I did worry if they would turn me away because it was my fault Douglass was dead.

&

Dear Diary,

Date and time unknown

>*This will be our last conversation. I feel the end is near. I can barely hold you and the pencil in which I use to communicate with you. I'm sorry we don't have many more years together. I hope I didn't disappoint you by ending things this way but I just could not live with the guilt of Douglass' death. When my family finds us cuddled together please tell them to bury you with me. In this life we have been best friends since I learn to write and I'm hoping we can remain best friends in my next life. Diary I love you and always will. Forgive me.*

Love Kim

&

My right hand, now constantly in pain and pouring brown thick liquid the consistency of ketchup, somehow managed to hold on to a pencil the size of my pinky long enough to say my good-byes. With tears clouding my vision I managed to convey my last words and wishes to the only best friend I ever had. I was ready to invade a world I have been working hard to enter. I was at peace with what was happening to my body, I was at peace with leaving this world, I was at peace with never speaking an Earthly word again. My eyes then closed.

Chapter 19

A New Life

"**W**ake up, young lady, wake up." A voice said.

Slowly opening my eyes, I was barely able to make out a multitude of shadows. I had no idea what these shadows were or even why they were huddled around me. At the time, I assumed I was in Heaven and the voice I heard was an angel welcoming me to the Pearly gates. But I thought to myself, shouldn't I be able to see this angel, shouldn't I be able to make out her pretty face.

Thinking this was normal I was ecstatic to know that I could let Douglass know just how sorry I was for what I had done to him. Not only that, I could tell Marcus just how stupid he was for running from the police and getting himself shot. I was prepared to tell them both just how I felt. But then I thought, after telling them what was on my mind then what. I was stuck up there with nothing to do. There's no Double Dutch, there's no *Good Humor* ice cream, there's no *Twilight Zone*. "Man" I thought "what had I done".

"Kim, wake up." A voice said.

Gradually, I realized this wasn't Heaven, that some-how I was still alive. And that voice, that voice belonged to the women who drove me crazy the most, The Queen.

"Come on Kim, wake-up." A tiny voice said.

Realizing the source of this voice was that of the one person I missed the most I began straining to focus on the blurred images around me. Just as the sun rose each morning to reveal a new day my blurred eyes opened to reveal a new chapter in my life. Once my vision completely returned, I was amazed to see my entire family huddled around me as I laid flat on an unknown bed.

Attempting to use my right hand to wipe my eyes and get an even clearer view of my family members' faces I noticed it was bandaged from the tips of my fingers to half-way up my skinny arm. I had no sensation in my hand. Convinced that it was no longer a part of my body I began crying hysterically as I attempted to remove the badges.

"Young lady, don't remove the badges." A lady said.

"Leave me alone. What have you done with my hand? You cut it off didn't you, didn't you?" I screamed.

"No young lady, we didn't cut off your hand. It's just bandaged to help fight the infections." She continued.

"You're lying, you're lying." I screamed even louder.

"Kimberly, you'll fine." A strong voice said.

Turning my head in the direction of the voice and focusing on the source of the statement I realized everything was okay. I knew when my father said something it was the truth so I calmed down, laid back and closed my eyes in relief.

"Kim, are you okay? Hey, it's me Kevin." A tiny voice said.

"Now, don't strain." A lady who I later identified as a nurse said noticing my strain to move toward Kevin.

"You're going to be okay." She continued.

After taking several seconds to relax I then gave Kevin the biggest smile I could make. I then panned the room to notice my mother, sisters, Mr. Parkinston, my aunt and uncle and grandmother. That was everyone except Douglass.

Waking up in what was later identified as Provident hospital and seeing the faces of my family sent chills down my spine. With everything I put myself through, with all the cries of ending it all I was grateful to find I was still alive. Deep down I knew I didn't want to end my life but for irrelevant reasons I continued with my quest anyway.

"Kim, I'm so glad you're okay. You had me worried sick." My mother said.

"Yeah, you little brat. I didn't have anybody to bother." Kathy said.

"Kimberly, you have to hurry up and get strong because we have a lot of time to make up for." Mr. Parkinston said.

"Young lady." The Nurse said.

"We're going to keep you in the hospital over-night then you can go home with your family tomorrow. " She continued.

"But we don't have a home." I blurted out.

"Kim, your family is living with me until your parents settle on your new home." Uncle Marvin said.

"Wait a minute" I thought to myself, "he said a word I had never heard in reference to me before, parents."

"What do you mean?" I struggled to ask.

"Well, since your house was destroyed your mother and father have been searching for a new place for you guys to live in. They finally found the perfect place in Northwest Baltimore." Uncle Marvin continued.

"It's a nice house." Kevin said.

"We're moving to Belle Ave. off of Garrison Blvd. You know right up the street from Garrison Junior High school." My mother, who I barely recognized because she was not sporting that blue scarf said.

"It has lots of trees and grass and a big back yard. We can play baseball anytime we want now." Kevin said.

"What?" I said thinking this was some type of dream. I couldn't believe it, a house with a big yard.

"Kimberly, I think you, your mother, sisters and brother will be very happy in the new house." Mr. Parkinston said.

"Did Douglass die?" I said after a brief pause.

I could tell by the expressions on every person in the room that I lost the brother I blamed so much of my agony on. I couldn't believe it; I was hoping this was just a bad dream and that I would wake up and he would be at the foot of my bed smiling and teasing me.

"Douglass is not with the Lord now. After you left, he joined the Army. We called him to let him know that you were found. He said to tell that stupid little sister of mine that I love her and I will see you soon." My mother explained.

"Kim, I'm so glad the Police found you when they did. We have been looking everywhere for you. My God I thought you had been killed or kidnapped or something. I don't know what I would have done if something would have happened to you. I love you so much, I know I've always been hard on you but it was because I had to toughen you up. This world would have swallowed you up and spit you out. You were entirely too trusting and, and you gave into any and everybody's demands entirely too easy. But I saw you grow, I saw you stand up to people. Like that Mr. Shipiro and eventually me.

I know now that you will be able to handle yourself, you now know how to stand up for yourself. And Kimberly, if you ever find yourself doubting your strength just think about how you stood up to me and Douglass. You know, it was because of you that he began to change his life. I was so proud of you when you stood up to him that I just cried. " My mother proudly said.

Chapter 20

My New Beginning

I returned to school on a warm June day and was enthusiastically welcomed by my teachers and classmates. My best friend Darlene had not yet returned to school but rumours were that she would someday walk again and she just may be able to join our Double Dutch team. The school had allowed Darlene to do all her work from home. The other members of my Double Dutch team, Niecy and Debbie, had joined forces with Operation Champ to provide lessons to kids all over the city. Graduation was just three days away when I was called to Mr. Bradford's, my eighth-grade counsellor, office.

"Come in Kimberly." He said as I approached the door to his office.

"You wanted to see me."

"Yes Kimberly. Have a seat." He replied.

"Yes sir." I said as I sat down.

"So, how are you? We'll all glad you are okay."

"I'm fine thank you." I said nervously.

"Don't be nervous. I have good news for you.

Over the next two days I need you to work on a Valedictorian speech to your classmates, family and friends."

"What?"

"Yes, you are the only student with a perfect "A" average. The salutatorian, Darlene Montgomery earned all A's in all her classes except one where she earned a B+. It was close, but you're our number one student for the class of 1968."

"Yes!" I said ecstatically.

"I'm sorry." I apologized.

"No need to apologize, but there is more good news. Your performance on the scholarship test has earned you a spot in Western High school's accelerated program. The program is just as good as that in which your sister Beatrice is in and you don't have to wear a uniform. But you will have to continue to work very hard to stay in the program because you must maintain a B average. Is that okay with you?"

"Yes sir, yes sir." I said enthusiastically.

"Okay so I will see you on graduation day, sitting on stage next to me."

"Okay" I said as I quickly stood up and headed toward the door.

"Wait a minute, don't leave so quickly."

"But I have to tell my mother and Mr. Parkinston." I said.

"I mean my father" I said after smiling and thinking to myself.

"Okay, go ahead."

Later that evening, as the entire family sat around Uncle Marvin's living room eating a feast made for a King, I found myself happier than I had been in years. It was great listening to all the family stories, most of which about my mother. Not surprisingly she was a handful coming up. I don't see how Uncle Marvin and my two aunts Mary and Tinie survived the constant harassment of the practical joker.

"Kimberly." My grandmother said.

"Yes" I answered.

"You know how hard your mother was on you. That was nothing, I used to ride your mother so much I don't believe a second went by when I was correcting her for one thing or another. Not that it did any good." She continued.

"Oh come on, it did some good. It's just that I didn't learn. But I did later." My mother said.

"Whatever you say." My grandmother said chuckling.

"Mom, that's not fair." My mother said taking out a cigarette.

"See." My grandmother said smiling.

"Okay, okay, I'll put it away." My mother said putting the cigarette in her pocketbook.

"You know Mom, I believe everything grandmother said." Douglass said hugging my mother as he was home from Boot Camp.

"Thanks." My mother said as she stared at the floor.

"Guess what." I said

"Yes Kim." My grandmother replied.

"I'm the valedictorian."

"What?" My mother said after getting up and giving me the tightest hung she had ever given a person before.

"Oh my baby, I just knew you could do it. With all the Hell I put you through you continued to do well. I'm so proud of you." She continued.

&

After working hard for two long days on my Valedictorian speech graduation day had finally arrived. From my seat on the raised stage I could see that the school's auditorium was filled with hundreds of proud parents, families and friends. The first few rows were reserved for teachers, administrators and the families of the valedictorian and salutatorian.

Seated in the front were all my sisters, brothers, uncle, aunts, cousins, grandmother, mother and most proudly my father. Next to them sat Mr. and Mrs. Montgomery and Darlene's older brother James. Despite the events of the recent past the two families embraced each other's presence.

I could see the smiles and hear the laughter as they discussed whatever it was they were talking about. At one-point Mrs. Montgomery actually walked to my mother and gave her a big hug.

Minutes before the ceremony began the back-stage curtain opened to reveal Darlene in a wheel chair. Happy to see my good friend I quickly got out of my chair and ran to her.

"Kim!" She said in tears.

"Darlene!" I said trying to hold back my tears.

"I'm so glad you are okay. I was so worried about you. Where were you?" Darlene asked.

"I'll tell you all about it later. Come on I'll take you on stage. You're going to sit next to me." I said walking behind the wheel chair.

"I'm so glad we are the top two. Me and my best friend on stage together." Darlene said.

As I pushed the wheel chair on stage the vast audience became gravely silent, then suddenly members of the audience began standing and cheering us on. After several minutes of loud cheers, the crowd silenced as the principle, Mrs. Sworn, walked on stage and took her place behind the podium.

"Good evening friends and parents of the graduating class of 1968."

"Yay!!" The crowd screamed before the introduction of several special guest and keynote speakers. Listening to them was long and boring but I somehow managed to stay awake despite not hearing a word they said. With the conclusion of each speaker my nerves intensified. By the final speaker, I was unsure if I could give the speech I worked so hard on.

It was now my turn; the principle had just introduced me as the Valedictorian and the crowd was now awaiting my speech. Looking at Darlene for support and Darlene looking at me as if to say "It's okay" I confidently made my way to the podium.

"Parents, friends and classmates welcome to the graduation exercises for the class of 1968 of Division Junior High school." I said as the crowd cheered.

"Today is a happy day for all of us. It's the first day we can say that we have made our way through the doors of junior high school and are now ready to walk the halls of high school. "

"Yay!!!" The members of the graduating class cheered.

"This three-year journey has been difficult; it has been fun and it has given me some of the best times of my life. But this three-year journey has personally given me some of the most difficult times of my life, especially the last six months. "I continued as the crowd came to a complete silence.

"During this time, I really learned a lot about myself. I went from a pony-tail wearing innocent little eighth grader to a wise intolerant teenager. I was the naïve fifth child in a large family. I always considered myself lost in this strange world. I had no idea who I wanted to be or even what type of person I dreamed of being as an adult. At times, I hated myself and I hated the life I was given. At times life was unbearable, at times life was confusing, at times life was terrifying. Unable to handle the loses suffered during this time I wanted to end it all. So, I tried. (Pause) So I tried because I felt I let my family and myself down. (Pause) But thank God I failed. I failed to leave this world in a manner in which the Holy Father frowned upon. And for the first time in my life I was glad to call myself a failure. Had I accomplished my goal I would not be standing in front of all of you good people accepting my position as the 1968 Valedictorian of this fine school. "I read before the crowd stood up and cheered.

While the cheering continued Darlene looked happily at me and we then approached each other, then hugged. The crowd then stood to their feet and began clapping as we embraced. As the cheers slowly subsided, I again took my place behind the podium.

"Principle Sworn, I am now turning the Class of 1968 over to you." I ended.

Principle Sworn continued the graduation ceremony, bringing the end to my stay as a shy gullible little girl.

&

July arrived in Baltimore just like any other year, hot and muggy. Most of the city's residents were preparing for the upcoming July 4th celebrations and we were no exception as my mother, brothers, sisters and I had recently moved into our gigantic new home on Belle Ave. A two-story home with a large living room and dining room it had enough bedrooms for the entire family to sleep comfortably. My mother's and Mae's room and the room I shared with Naomi were on the first floor. On the second floor were two very large rooms, one for Douglass, Kevin and Lamar and the other for Kathy and Beatrice.

After my two weeks in Druid Hill park I was grateful to be alive and cherished every minute with my sisters, mother, brothers and happy to say father. Thought my parents lived in separate quarters I still had a since of family as Mr. Parkinston spent many hours ensuring my mother was prepared to purchase her dream home. He gave her advice as well as money and a sense of confidence. His persona and great love for life had a calming effect on Mom as well as my formally dysfunctional family. Our now high-energy cohesive pile of puzzle pieces now made a jagged free image once again. The image was now glossy and easy to make out; And to my surprise my mother had not worn that awful blue scarf since I returned home.

We moved into our new home on June 30, 1968. I couldn't believe how large the house was. As you entered the front door you entered into the large living room with the largest fireplace I had ever seen. To the back of the living room was a large Dining room that had three exits. The first exit was on the left and was a hallway that led to several first-floor bedrooms and the bathroom. The second exit was a staircase that led to the two upstairs bedrooms and the third exit was to the kitchen which contained a large pantry.

I was excited when Mr. Parkinson and Douglass drove up in a truck with all the things from our house on Preston Street. There were many boxes of stuff, the dinette set, all the bedroom furniture except my mom's and most importantly the dresser in which I kept my best friend. As we unpacked the many boxes, I began hearing a strange noise. Not having an idea as to where the noise was coming from I thought that it was from some sort of animal that had gotten into the house and was trying to get out. As we continued unpacking the sound got louder and louder. We looked all over the place for the source of the noise.

"What is that noise?" Beatrice said in a frighten voice.

"I don't know." My Mom replied.

"Mommy, I'm scared." Beatrice said.

"You will be okay my love." My Mom said after walking to Beatrice and giving her a tight secure hug.

"Let's just continue to unpack." Naomi said trying to take our minds off the scary noise.

After unpacking several more boxes I reached one with the word "Livingroom" written on the top. When I picked up the box, I realized that the scary noise was coming from that box.

"The noise is coming from this box." I said

"I don't know if I should open it." I continued.

"Here, I'll opened it." Douglass said after taking the box.

After stretching his arms, cuffing his hands and cracking his fingers Douglass looks at us with the biggest smile and begins un-taping the box. Once opened Douglass slowly pulls out the contents of the box, that pain in the butt clock. I should have known. I couldn't believe it, that clock had more lives than a cat.

Christening of our new home was set for July 4th. Our former neighbours and friends from Preston Street along with my Uncles, aunts, cousins and grandmother were all invited to the celebration. This event was to signal the end of a difficult year and the start of an enriching future. It was to be the party of the century.

July 4th arrived and it took every bit of four days to prepare the house and yard for the great event. When 2:00 p.m. approached, the grill was fired up and the guest began arriving. By 4:00 p.m. there were more than fifty people enjoying the food and games in the backyard.

The older kids ran back and forth between the badminton game and the food stations while the younger kids chased each other in circles. As expected, the adults sat endlessly stuffing their faces with hot dogs, hamburgers, barbecue chicken, corn on the cob, potato salad, chips and a host of other foods. Darlene, still recuperating in a wheelchair, spent most of her time with her brother and parents at the adult table.

"Hey Darlene wanna play cards?" I asked.

"No not really."

"We can play crazy 8s."

"No I don't feel like it."

"Well what if we played hangman, I can get some paper and a couple of pencils."

"No, I don't want to." Darlene said angrily.

"Well, okay" I said sensing a cold enormous wedge between the two of us.

"Why don't you go back and play with the others. If I want to play a game or something I'll call you." Darlene said in an attempt to push me away.

"Well okay." I said trying to hold back the tears as I realized what she was doing.

"Okay everybody." My mother yelled as I began walking away.

"It's time to bless our new home. So, let's all form a circle on the patio." She continued.

As instructed the happy crowd gathered on the patio and formed a large circle. I stood with Darlene to the right, Kevin to my left and my father to the left of him. To the right of Darlene was her mother, father, brother then Douglass, Uncle Marvin then my grandmother and Pastor Clemson. The remainder of the circle consisted of the numerous friends, including Mrs. Wilson, and extended family members.

"Let's all hold hands and bow our heads." Pastor Clemson said. The crowd happily obeys.

"Dear Lord we would like to take this time to bless this home at 4010 Belle avenue where a special family has just moved. Lord please ensure that this new home gives this family many safe and happy times and protect this home from all Earthly evils. Let everybody say amen." Pastor Clemson said.

"Amen!" The crowd said loudly.

"Now before you guys go back to the great food Delores and her fine family have prepared, I would like Delores Carter and Calvin Parkinston to come before me. "Pastor Clemons said.

Unaware of what the Pastor had in mind I watched my mother and father make their way in front of the Pastor. As the two approached the Pastor they stopped and looked into each other eyes then began gently holding hands.

"I love you." I heard my father say to my mother.

"I love you too." My mother said.

"As some of you may have guest by now my dear friends Delores and Calvin would like you to witness the union of their marriage." The Pastor explained.

"What!" I happily said.

"You're kidding." Beatrice said as the crowd began cheering and whispering to each other.

"Calm down." The Pastor said.

"Now, let's get started." The Pastor continued.

After several minutes of loving vowels, I finally had the complete family I always wanted. I couldn't believe it, not only did I have a father but I had a mother and father who were married and were ready to live together in our new home as a family.

"This was a dream come true" I thought to myself as I watched my parents kiss.

"Kim." A voice said bringing me out of my trance.

"Yeah." I said realizing the voice was that of Darlene.

"I'm sorry I acted so cold to you earlier." Darlene said.

"Oh, I'm not mad at you."

"Well you should be. I shouldn't have ignored you like that." She said as the crowd disbanded.

"My parents and I talked to my doctor yesterday and he gave me some bad news." Darlene continued.

"What did he say?" I said curiously.

"He said that the chances of me walking again were very slim." Darlene said.

"Oh my God." I said.

"It's okay. I'll just have to live with it." Darlene said trying to hold back the tears.

Though she fought hard to hold in the tears her emotions got the best of her and she burst into an uncontrollable cry. She then backed up and rolled the chair toward her parents. Before reaching the table in which they were sitting she stopped, turned to face me, stared and wiped a few tears from her eyes.

Darlene's life sentence instantly took the joy of the day and turned it into a sorrow filled event. It's amazing how a girl who had all the right ingredients for a promising future now had a major obstacle in her quest. Needing to digest Darlene's fate I decided to go in the house and leave the happy crowd. As I walked in the living room and sat on the sofa facing the fireplace, I looked around the room thinking about the last few months.

My future, which earlier that year seemed bleak, now seemed promising as my whole world had come together to form that perfect image. I couldn't help smiling and giggling about all my adventures. I even thought about the incident with the bleeder; But I found nothing funny about that incident and to this day I still hate that ugly nose bleeding idiot.

After several minutes of deep thought the ticking of that stupid clock distracted me, forcing me to come back to the real word. I was so pissed that I grabbed a hammer from the kitchen drawer and headed straight for that annoying thing. As I raised the hammer, ready to hit the clock into a million pieces, I stopped. I just couldn't do it. After years of wanting that thing gone, I just couldn't kill it.

"Dag", I thought.

"I guess my compassion for mankind transferred to that stupid clock. Man that sucks" I thought as the Queen walked in, stopped and shook her head as she noticed the criminal act I was about to commit.

"I was just tryin' to fix the second hand." I said lowering the hammer.

The Queen rolls her eyes and continues to the couch where she sits slowly staring brainlessly out the nearby window.

Her expression was one I had seen many times. It was one of deep depression as she thought about an abandonment she had never forgotten.

"I'm sure your mother had a reason for leaving you." I said as I sat on her right side while putting my left hand on top of her right hand.

R.C. McDonald

R.C. McDonald grew up in the city of Baltimore to a family of four boys, herself, parents and an extended family. She attended the Baltimore City public Schools, having graduated from Forest Park High school. Later she attended Morgan State University where she graduated with a B.S. in Mathematics then one year later a B.S. in Computer Science. She went on to earn a M.S. in Computer Science from Bowie State University and an MBA from the University of Maryland. She has enjoyed working in the technical field for several government agencies including NASA.

Ms. McDonald's love for writing began as a child. She would write short stories in her spare time but never tried to pursue writing more seriously. As an adult she began taking writing a bit more seriously as she managed to complete her first book. Again, she had no intentions of doing anything with the book but with the encouragement of friends and family she researched the best methods to publishing the book and followed through. Ms. McDonald enjoys the publishing industry so much she has recently started her own publishing company, Nicholson & fisher. The company is currently in the infancy stage but Ms. McDonald has set goals for growing the business.

Ms. McDonald is currently working on several novels, an historical fiction based on Complex Puzzle book, an Anthology of short stories of strong female characters and the beginnings of a Mystery series. Ms.

McDonald loves to write historical fictions with strong female characters and plans on publishing her second books by the end of 2020.

Ms. McDonald works many hours tutoring children in Math and the sciences as she believes the kids are the future. As she wrote Complex Puzzle, Ms. McDonald realized that all kids, despite their living conditions as a child, can succeed as adults. This philosophy and her love for history are the basis for all her work.

Made in the USA
Middletown, DE
25 July 2020